D1466032

salad suppers
15 minute main dish meals

by Theresa Millang

Adventure Publications, Inc.
Cambridge, MN

Thank you

A special thank you to friends, family and all other contributors to this collection.

Edited by Dan Downing
Cover and book design by Lora Westberg

10 9 8 7 6 5 4 3 2 1

Copyright 2012 by Theresa Nell Millang
Published by Adventure Publications, Inc.
820 Cleveland Street South
Cambridge, Minnesota 55008
1-800-678-7006
www.adventurepublications.net
All rights Reserved
Printed in China
ISBN: 978-1-59193-349-6

Table of Contents

Beef

Vegetarian

Introduction

Today's busy people are looking for fast, easy-to-prepare homemade food for their families. In this collection of recipes, there are countless ways to create meals perfect for everyday eating and even special occasions.

Salad Suppers will show you how to prepare these meals in 15 minutes of cooking time or less.

This collection is presented in six categories: Chicken, Turkey, Seafood, Beef, Pork and Vegetarian. Featured are contemporary and classic recipes prepared on stove-top, by broiling and indoor and outdoor grilling, and even without cooking.

Choose cold or warm salads and enjoy delicious meals such as Cashew Chicken Salad, Fresh Salmon Pasta Salad, Couscous Turkey Salad, Pork Taco Salad, Beef Fajita Salad, Edamame Pasta Salad and so many more.

I hope you will enjoy this collection of recipes. I have added my favorite recipes and recipes from family and friends from across the country.

chicken

Asian Chicken Orange Salad

INGREDIENTS

Dressing

3 tablespoons white vinegar or unflavored rice vinegar

2 tablespoons soy sauce

2 tablespoons honey

2 tablespoons vegetable oil

1 tablespoon toasted sesame oil

Salad

8 cups torn romaine lettuce

1 8-ounce can water chestnuts, drained

1 small red onion, thinly sliced, divided

1 small orange, peeled and sectioned

3 cups sliced cooked rotisserie chicken

¼ teaspoon ground black pepper, or to taste

1 cup chow mein noodles

1 teaspoon sesame seeds, toasted

6 SERVINGS

Mix all salad dressing ingredients in a small container until blended.

Mix lettuce, water chestnuts and half the red onion in a bowl. Arrange on a large serving platter. Top decoratively with remaining onion, orange sections and chicken. Sprinkle with black pepper as desired.

Drizzle salad with dressing and sprinkle with chow mein noodles and sesame seeds. Serve. Refrigerate leftovers.

Use an 11-ounce can of Mandarin oranges, drained, in place of fresh orange, if desired. Serve with rice crackers.

One serving contains approximately: Calories 267, Fat 11g, Carbohydrates 17g, Protein 24g

Asian Chicken Rice Salad

Whisk olive oil, lemon juice, soy sauce, ginger and teriyaki sauce in a small container. Stir in salt and black pepper to taste.

Combine rice, chicken, celery, water chestnuts, mushrooms, green onions, bell pepper and carrots in a large bowl. Add salad dressing; stir to coat well. Cover and chill slightly. Serve. Refrigerate leftovers.

Cooked rice can be found in the freezer section of your supermarket. Serve with crisp breadsticks. Garnish each serving with sliced fresh cucumbers.

One serving contains approximately: Calories 232, Fat 7g, Carbohydrates 26g, Protein 17g

INGREDIENTS

2 tablespoons extra virgin olive oil

3 tablespoons fresh lemon juice

3 tablespoons reduced-sodium soy sauce

1 teaspoon minced fresh ginger root

1 teaspoon teriyaki sauce

Salt and ground black pepper to taste

4 cups cooked brown rice, cold

2 cups chopped cooked rotisserie chicken breast

1 cup sliced celery

1 cup sliced water chestnuts

1 cup sliced fresh button mushrooms

½ cup diced green onions

½ cup diced red bell pepper

⅓ cup matchstick-size fresh carrots

6 SERVINGS

Asian Noodle Chicken Salad

INGREDIENTS

1 16-ounce package 3-color coleslaw blend

2 tablespoons sliced green onions

1 9-ounce package frozen fully cooked chicken breast strips, thawed

⅓ cup citrus-flavored vinaigrette salad dressing

1 3-ounce package Oriental-flavor ramen noodle soup mix

5 SERVINGS

Mix coleslaw, onions, chicken and salad dressing in a large bowl.

Discard seasoning packet from soup mix. Coarsely crush the noodles and add to salad; stir gently to mix. Serve immediately. Refrigerate leftovers.

A tri-color coleslaw blend is used in this quick salad.

One serving contains approximately: Calories 210, Fat 6g, Carbohydrates 20g, Protein 19g

Avocado Chicken Salad

Place all ingredients in a large bowl; toss gently to coat well. Serve immediately. Refrigerate leftovers.

Serve this quick meal with warm hard rolls.

One serving contains approximately: Calories 190, Fat 5g, Carbohydrates 15g, Protein 5g

INGREDIENTS

1 firm ripe avocado, peeled, pitted and diced

2 cups shredded cooked rotisserie chicken breast

½ cup sliced green onion

1 4-ounce package mixed baby salad greens

½ cup fat-free balsamic vinaigrette

4 SERVINGS

Basil Pesto Chicken Salad

INGREDIENTS

½ cup mayonnaise

½ cup purchased basil pesto

½ teaspoon salt

¼ teaspoon ground black pepper

1 2-pound cooked rotisserie chicken, skin and bones discarded and meat coarsely chopped

6 cups arugula or chopped romaine hearts

Grape tomatoes, optional

4 SERVINGS

Mix mayonnaise, pesto, salt and black pepper in a large bowl. Stir in chicken to coat. Serve over salad greens. Garnish with grape tomatoes as desired. Refrigerate leftovers.

Serve with hard rolls.

One serving contains approximately: Calories 627, Fat 47g, Carbohydrates 3g, Protein 47g

Black Beans Chicken Pasta Salad

Cook pasta according to package directions. Rinse with cold water in a colander and drain well. Place in a large bowl.

Add chicken, cheese, tomatoes, bell pepper and beans to bowl; toss.

Mix salad dressing, lemon juice and Tabasco sauce in a small container. Add to salad mixture; mix well. Cover and chill slightly before serving. Refrigerate leftovers.

Serve over leaf lettuce along with warm rolls.

One serving contains approximately: Calories 470, Fat 26g, Carbohydrates 34g, Protein 25g

INGREDIENTS

1 cup uncooked medium pasta shells

1½ cups cubed cooked skinless rotisserie chicken breast

1 cup cubed Cheddar cheese

1 cup cherry tomatoes, halved

1 small green bell pepper, cut into thin strips, then cut in half

1 15-ounce can black beans, rinsed and drained

⅔ cup Italian salad dressing

2 tablespoons fresh lemon juice

¼ teaspoon Tabasco sauce

5 SERVINGS

Bow Ties with Sausage Salad

INGREDIENTS

¾ **pound uncooked dry bow tie pasta**

1 **tablespoon extra virgin olive oil**

1 **pound Italian chicken sausage, casings removed, meat crumbled**

4 **jarred roasted red peppers, cut into thin strips**

8 **ounces baby spinach**

½ **teaspoon red pepper flakes, crushed**

2 **tablespoons low-sodium chicken broth**

½ **cup grated Parmesan cheese**

4 SERVINGS

Cook pasta according to package directions; drain in a colander.

Heat olive oil in a large nonstick skillet over medium heat. Add sausage; stir and cook until no longer pink, about 4 minutes. Stir in peppers. Add spinach; stir until wilted. Remove skillet from heat. Add pepper flakes, broth and drained cooked pasta; mix well.

Place equal amounts of mixture into 4 salad bowls. Sprinkle each equally with Parmesan cheese. Serve. Refrigerate leftovers.

Serve this warm with garlic toast.

One serving contains approximately: Calories 590, Fat 15, Carbohydrates 80g, Protein 31g

Buffalo Chicken Salad

Heat oil in a medium nonstick skillet over medium heat. Place chicken flat in skillet. Cook, turning once, until golden brown and cooked through, about 10 minutes. Cool. Tear meat into thick shreds and place in a small bowl. Add hot sauce; toss.

Toss lettuce, celery and salad dressing in a large bowl. Place on a dinner plate. Top with chicken, blue cheese and a few croutons. Serve immediately. Refrigerate leftovers.

Double the recipe . . . and share this tasty meal with a friend.

One serving contains approximately: Calories 440, Fat 30g, Carbohydrates 11g, Protein 30g

INGREDIENTS

2 teaspoons cooking oil

2 boneless skinless chicken thighs, lightly seasoned with salt and black pepper

2 teaspoons hot sauce, more if desired

3 cups roughly chopped romaine lettuce

2 ribs celery, sliced

2 tablespoons light ranch salad dressing, more if desired

½ ounce blue cheese, crumbled

Croutons

1 SERVING

California Chicken Salad

INGREDIENTS

2 pounds boneless skinless cooked chicken breast, diced

¾ cup pecan pieces, toasted

2 cups red seedless grapes

3 ribs celery, thinly sliced

Dressing

1 cup mayonnaise

4 teaspoons apple cider vinegar

5 teaspoons honey

2 teaspoons poppy seeds

¼ teaspoon salt, or to taste

⅛ teaspoon ground black pepper

6 SERVINGS

Mix chicken, pecans, grapes and celery in a large bowl.

Mix all salad dressing ingredients in a small bowl until well blended. Pour over chicken mixture; stir to combine. Serve. Refrigerate leftovers.

Serve over butter lettuce along with warm soft rolls.

One serving contains approximately: Calories 610, Fat 43g, Carbohydrates 17g, Protein 33g

Cashew Chicken Salad

Remove meat with your hands, tearing into bite-size pieces. Place in a large bowl. Add celery, cashews and onion.

Mix remaining ingredients in a small container until blended; stir into chicken mixture. Chill slightly. Refrigerate leftovers

Serve over leafy greens along with warm croissants or buttered rolls.

One serving contains approximately: Calories 250, Fat 20g, Carbohydrates 10g, Protein 19g

INGREDIENTS

1 cooked rotisserie chicken, cold, skin and bones discarded

1 cup chopped celery

¾ cup chopped cashews

½ cup minced red onion

¾ cup light sour cream

¼ cup mayonnaise

2 tablespoons fresh lemon juice

¾ teaspoon dried tarragon

¼ teaspoon salt, or to taste

¼ teaspoon ground black pepper

6 SERVINGS

Chicken and Bacon Orzo Salad

INGREDIENTS

1½ cups uncooked dried orzo pasta

2 cups cooked cubed chicken

2 cups halved grape tomatoes

2 cups packed fresh baby spinach
   leaves

½ cup sliced green onions

1 tablespoon chopped pitted
   kalamata olives

4 strips bacon, crisply cooked,
   drained and crumbled

3 tablespoons extra virgin olive oil

1½ tablespoons white vinegar

½ teaspoon Dijon mustard

¼ teaspoon coarse salt

¼ teaspoon freshly ground
   black pepper

5 SERVINGS

Cook pasta according to package directions; drain and rinse under running cold water, then drain again. Place in a large bowl.

Add chicken, tomatoes, spinach, onions, olives and bacon to pasta.

Mix remaining ingredients in a small container until blended; add to chicken mixture and toss until coated. Refrigerate leftovers.

Orzo pasta resembles large grains of rice.

One serving contains approximately: Calories 350, Fat 14g, Carbohydrates 30g, Protein 25g

Chicken BLT Salad

Toss all ingredients in a large bowl. Chill slightly before serving. Refrigerate leftovers.

Top each serving with croutons.

One serving contains approximately: Calories 270, Fat 14g, Carbohydrates 7g, Protein 29g

INGREDIENTS

2 cups shredded cooked rotisserie chicken

8 slices bacon, crisply cooked, drained and chopped

8 cups chopped romaine lettuce

1 cup halved cherry tomatoes

¼ cup ranch salad dressing

⅓ cup shredded four-cheese blend

4 SERVINGS

Chicken Broccoli Pasta Salad

INGREDIENTS

1½ cups uncooked rotini pasta

1 cup cubed cooked skinless rotisserie chicken breast

2 cups fresh broccoli florets

Half of a green bell pepper, chopped

Half of a red bell pepper, chopped

1 small red onion, finely chopped

¾ cup fat-free Italian salad dressing

6 SERVINGS

Cook pasta according to package directions; drain in a colander and rinse with cold water then drain again. Place in a large bowl.

Add all remaining ingredients to bowl. Cover and chill slightly. Serve. Refrigerate leftovers.

Garnish with fresh tomato wedges. Serve with warm garlic bread.

One serving contains approximately: Calories 200, Fat 2g, Carbohydrates 31g, Protein 3g

Chicken Brown Rice Salad

Mix all ingredients except lettuce in a large bowl. Cover and chill slightly. Stir in lettuce just before serving. Refrigerate leftovers.

Rotisserie chicken and microwave rice make this meal quick to prepare.

One serving contains approximately: Calories 280, Fat 13g, Carbohydrates 24g, Protein 16g

INGREDIENTS

1 8.8-ounce package Hinode precooked brown rice, microwaved and chilled

2 cups coarsely shredded cooked skinless rotisserie chicken breast

¾ cup olive oil vinaigrette

½ cup chopped celery

½ cup chopped bell pepper

½ cup chopped green onion

1 tablespoon chopped flat-leaf parsley

1 cup coarsely chopped romaine lettuce or spinach

4 SERVINGS

Chicken Caesar Salad

INGREDIENTS

16 ounces boneless skinless fresh
   chicken breast

½ teaspoon salt

¼ teaspoon ground black pepper

¼ cup olive oil

3 fresh garlic cloves, minced

4 cups torn romaine lettuce

2 tablespoons fresh lemon juice

1 cup garlic-flavored croutons

¼ cup grated Parmesan cheese

8 whole anchovy fillets, optional

Shaved Parmesan cheese, optional

4 SERVINGS

Cut chicken into 1-inch by ¼-inch strips; sprinkle with salt and pepper.

Heat olive oil in a large nonstick skillet over medium-high heat until hot. Add chicken and garlic; cook and stir frequently until chicken is cooked, about 5 minutes.

Place lettuce in a large shallow bowl. Add cooked chicken mixture, including oil, and lemon juice; toss. Add croutons and grated cheese; toss until well combined.

Place equal amounts of salad mixture on 4 plates. Garnish each, as desired, with anchovy fillets and shaved Parmesan cheese. Serve immediately. Refrigerate leftovers.

Fresh chicken breast is used in this salad.

One serving contains approximately: Calories 316, Fat 24, Carbohydrates 13g, Protein 32g

Chicken Couscous Salad

Pour boiling water over couscous in a saucepan; cover and let stand until absorbed. Spoon into a large bowl; fluff with a fork. Add chicken, tomatoes, onions, bell pepper, parsley, basil and lettuce to bowl; toss.

Mix salad dressing and garlic in a small container; add to bowl; mix well. Season with salt and black pepper to taste. Serve. Refrigerate leftovers.

Couscous cooks in minutes. Top salad with toasted nuts for crunch.

One serving contains approximately: Calories 270, Fat 11g, Carbohydrates 38g, Protein 10g

INGREDIENTS

1½ cups plain uncooked dry couscous

1½ cups boiling water

2 cups boneless skinless cooked rotisserie chicken

2 cups chopped fresh ripe tomatoes

2 green onions, thinly sliced

¼ cup chopped green bell pepper

¼ cup chopped fresh flat-leaf parsley

¼ cup chopped fresh basil

2 cups thinly sliced romaine lettuce

¼ cup Italian salad dressing

3 cloves crushed fresh garlic

Salt to taste

Ground black pepper to taste

8 SERVINGS

Chicken Gouda Cheese Salad

INGREDIENTS

2 cups diced skinless cooked rotisserie chicken, chilled

¼ cup small-diced red onion

4 slices bacon, cooked crisp, drained on paper towels

1 large Fuji apple, cored and cut into bite-size pieces

½ cup light olive oil vinaigrette

Mixed baby salad greens, optional

½ cup shaved aged Gouda cheese

4 SERVINGS

Mix chicken, onion, bacon and apple in a large bowl. Add vinaigrette; toss to coat well.

Line 4 salad plates with salad greens, if desired. Top each equally with chicken mixture and cheese. Serve. Refrigerate leftovers.

Variation: Shaved Parmesan cheese.

Serve with warm rolls.

One serving contains approximately: Calories 360, Fat 25g, Carbohydrates 13g, Protein 24g

Chicken Mango Salad

Toss chicken, mango, salad dressing, red onion and jerk seasoning in a bowl until coated.

Line 4 salad bowls equally with salad greens. Top each equally with chicken mixture. Serve. Refrigerate leftovers.

Top each serving with toasted slivered almonds. Serve with crusty bread.

One serving contains approximately: Calories 290, Fat 17g, Carbohydrates 21g, Protein 21g

INGREDIENTS

2 cups diced cooked rotisserie chicken

1 cup bite-size pieces fresh mango

⅔ cup light lime vinaigrette salad dressing

½ cup slivered red onion

1 teaspoon jerk seasoning

6 cups spring mix salad greens

4 SERVINGS

Chicken Salad with Peanut Butter Dressing

INGREDIENTS

3 cups diced cooked rotisserie chicken, cold

6 cups packaged coleslaw mix

3 cups fresh baby spinach leaves

1 medium green bell pepper, cut into ½-inch strips

1 8-ounce can bamboo shoots or sliced water chestnuts, rinsed and drained

Dressing

3 tablespoons soy sauce

3 tablespoons cider vinegar

2 tablespoons honey

1 tablespoon creamy peanut butter

½ teaspoon crushed red pepper flakes, or to taste

½ teaspoon grated ginger root

6 SERVINGS

Place chicken, coleslaw mix, spinach leaves, bell pepper and bamboo shoots in a large bowl.

Whisk all dressing ingredients in a small container. Drizzle over salad mixture; toss to coat. Serve. Refrigerate leftovers.

A quick Asian-type meal the whole family is sure to enjoy.

One serving contains approximately: Calories 210, Fat 5g, Carbohydrates 22g, Protein 23g

Chicken Salad with Pears

Mix all ingredients except salad greens in a medium bowl.

Line 4 plates with salad greens. Top each equally with salad mixture. Serve. Refrigerate leftovers.

Serve with soft bakery rolls.

One serving contains approximately: Calories 270, Fat 13g, Carbohydrates 14g, Protein 23g

INGREDIENTS

2 cups diced skinless rotisserie chicken breast

1 large firm ripe Bartlett pear, cut into bite-size pieces

½ cup thin strips of red bell pepper

⅓ cup coarsely chopped pecans, toasted

⅓ cup champagne salad dressing

2 small green onions, sliced

Spring mix salad greens

4 SERVINGS

Chicken Tortellini Salad

INGREDIENTS

1 9-ounce package cheese tortellini, cooked and cooled

1½ cups diced, cold rotisserie chicken meat, skin discarded

½ cup olive oil vinaigrette

½ cup halved cherry tomatoes

¼ cup sliced fresh basil

1 2.2-ounce can sliced ripe olives, drained

2 tablespoons chopped toasted walnuts

4 SERVINGS

Place all ingredients except walnuts in a medium bowl; stir gently to combine. Cover and chill slightly before serving. Sprinkle with walnuts just before serving.

Use balsamic vinaigrette instead of olive oil vinaigrette, if desired.

One serving contains approximately: Calories 350, Fat 17g, Carbohydrates 28g, Protein 21g

Chicken Wilted Lettuce Salad

Cook bacon in a small nonstick skillet over medium heat until crisp. Remove bacon; drain on paper towels. Reserve 1 tablespoon bacon drippings in saucepan; discard the rest.

Mix vinegar, mustard, olive oil, garlic, salt and pepper in a small container. Add to skillet; stir and bring to a boil. Remove from heat.

Pour hot mixture over romaine lettuce in a large bowl. Add chicken; toss until coated. Crumble bacon over top. Serve. Refrigerate leftovers.

Rotisserie chicken makes this meal easy to prepare. Garnish with grape tomatoes. Serve with warm rolls.

One serving contains approximately: Calories 240, Fat 15g, Carbohydrates 1g, Protein 24g

INGREDIENTS

4 slices bacon

2 tablespoons cider vinegar or red wine vinegar

1 tablespoon coarse Dijon mustard

1 tablespoon extra virgin olive oil

1 clove fresh garlic, crushed

¼ teaspoon salt

¼ teaspoon ground black pepper

1 9-ounce bag cut hearts of romaine lettuce

2 cups skinless, shredded cooked rotisserie chicken breast

4 SERVINGS

Chinese Chicken Noodle Salad

INGREDIENTS

1 tablespoon cooking oil

1 pound boneless skinless fresh chicken breast, cut crosswise into thin slices

6 ounces Chinese noodles, or 2 packages chicken-flavored ramen noodles, seasoning packet discarded

⅓ cup creamy peanut butter

1½ tablespoons red wine vinegar

3 tablespoons soy sauce

¼ cup water

1½ tablespoons granulated sugar

4 cups thinly sliced romaine lettuce strips

1 red bell pepper cut into thin strips

1 cup diced seedless cucumber

6 green onions, thinly sliced

6 SERVINGS

Heat oil in a large nonstick skillet over high heat. Add chicken; stir and cook until no longer pink and thoroughly cooked, about 5 minutes.

Cook noodles according to package directions. Drain in a colander; let cool.

Whisk peanut butter, vinegar, soy sauce, water and granulated sugar in a small container.

Mix chicken, noodles and peanut butter mixture in a large bowl until coated. Add remaining ingredients to bowl; toss. Serve immediately. Refrigerate leftovers.

Peanut butter runs through it!

One serving contains approximately: Calories 275, Fat 12g, Carbohydrates 22g, Protein 20g

Chipotle Chicken Salad

Put chicken, bell pepper, onions and cilantro in a large bowl.

Mix mayonnaise, chipotles, lime juice, salt and pepper in a small container. Add to chicken mixture; gently stir until combined. Chill slightly before serving. Refrigerate leftovers.

Serve on a bed of crisp lettuce along with warm hard rolls.

One serving contains approximately: Calories 360, Fat 22g, Carbohydrates 7g, Protein 31g

INGREDIENTS

4 cups coarsely shredded cooked skinless rotisserie chicken

1 red bell pepper, chopped

Half a large red onion, diced

3 green onions, thinly sliced

¼ cup chopped fresh cilantro or parsley

½ cup mayonnaise

¼ cup canned chipotles in adobo sauce, finely chopped

1 tablespoon fresh lime juice

½ teaspoon salt, or to taste

⅛ teaspoon ground black pepper

4 SERVINGS

Chipotle Chicken Taco Salad

INGREDIENTS

Salad

4 cups shredded romaine lettuce

2 cups coarsely shredded skinless rotisserie chicken breast

1 cup halved cherry tomatoes

1 ripe avocado, peeled, pitted and diced

Half a small red onion, thinly sliced and pulled into rings

1 15-ounce can black beans, rinsed and drained

1 cup canned whole kernel corn, rinsed and drained

Dressing

⅔ cup sour cream

⅓ cup chopped fresh cilantro

1 tablespoon finely chopped, canned chipotle chile pepper in adobo sauce

1 teaspoon chili powder

1 teaspoon ground cumin

1 tablespoon fresh lime juice

¼ teaspoon salt

4 SERVINGS

Place all salad ingredients in a large bowl; toss.

Stir all dressing ingredients in a small bowl; drizzle over salad mixture. Serve immediately. Refrigerate leftovers.

Variation: Use cooked shrimp instead of chicken. Serve with breadsticks.

One serving contains approximately: Calories 249, Fat 9g, Carbohydrates 25g, Protein 23g

Chopped Greek Chicken Salad

Place all dressing ingredients in a large bowl; whisk until blended.

Add chicken, tomato, cucumber, onion, olives and cheese to bowl. Toss to coat. Serve immediately. Refrigerate leftovers.

Serve with warm rolls.

One serving contains approximately: Calories 343, Fat 18g, Carbohydrates 11g, Protein 31g

INGREDIENTS

Dressing

2½ tablespoons red wine vinegar

1 tablespoon extra virgin olive oil

½ teaspoon dried oregano

½ teaspoon dried dill weed

½ teaspoon garlic powder

⅛ teaspoon salt

⅛ teaspoon ground black pepper

6 ounces chopped cooked chicken (about 1¼ cups)

1 ripe tomato, chopped

1 small cucumber, peeled, seeded and chopped

¼ cup finely chopped red onion

¼ cup sliced black olives

¼ cup crumbled feta cheese

2 SERVINGS

Cobb Salad

INGREDIENTS

Dressing

½ cup purchased blue cheese salad dressing

¾ cup crumbled blue cheese, divided

2 tablespoons fresh lemon juice, divided

½ teaspoon fresh lemon zest

12 cups shredded romaine lettuce

2 cups diced cooked rotisserie chicken breast

2 cups diced cooked deli roast beef

1 cup diced zucchini

1 ripe avocado, peeled, pitted and diced

4 plum tomatoes, diced

2 hard-boiled eggs, chopped

4 ounces thick-sliced bacon, cut into ½-inch pieces, cooked crisp

6 SERVINGS

Mix purchased blue cheese salad dressing, ¼ cup crumbled blue cheese, 1 tablespoon lemon juice and the lemon zest in a small container; pour into a small serving pitcher.

Toss lettuce with ¼ cup dressing mixture in a large bowl; place on a large serving platter.

In separate rows, arrange remaining ½ cup crumbled blue cheese, chicken, beef, zucchini, avocado, tomatoes, eggs and bacon on top of lettuce. Drizzle remaining lemon juice over avocado, tomatoes and zucchini. Pass remaining salad dressing when serving. Serve immediately. Refrigerate leftovers.

This is a great meal for a special night. Serve with warm rolls.

One serving contains approximately: Calories 406, Fat 28g, Carbohydrates 9g, Protein 31g

Couscous Chicken Salad

Bring broth to a boil in a 2-quart saucepan over medium-high heat. Stir in couscous. Remove saucepan from heat; cover and let stand 5 minutes. Fluff with a fork.

Whisk all dressing ingredients in a small container until blended.

Mix chicken, cucumbers, tomatoes, olives, cheese, parsley, salt and black pepper in a large bowl. Stir in cooked couscous. Add half the salad dressing to mixture. Toss, adding more salad dressing for your desired consistency. Serve. Refrigerate leftovers.

Variation: Use purchased white balsamic vinaigrette salad dressing.

One serving contains approximately: Calories 640, Fat 39g, Carbohydrates 44g, Protein 29g

INGREDIENTS

2 cups chicken broth

1 10-ounce box plain-flavor uncooked couscous

Dressing

¾ cup extra virgin olive oil

¼ cup fresh lemon juice

2 tablespoons white balsamic vinegar

¼ teaspoon crushed dried rosemary leaves

¼ teaspoon salt

2 cooked skinless rotisserie chicken breast halves, cubed

1 cup diced seedless cucumber

½ cup chopped sun-dried tomatoes

½ cup chopped black olives

½ cup crumbled feta cheese

⅓ cup chopped fresh flat-leaf parsley

¼ teaspoon salt

¼ teaspoon ground black pepper

6 SERVINGS

Creamy Fruited Chicken Pasta Salad

INGREDIENTS

4 cups uncooked bow tie pasta

1½ cups cubed cooked skinless rotisserie chicken breast

2 cups fresh strawberries, sliced

2 cups seedless red grapes, halved

2 cups fresh cantaloupe chunks

1 green onion, chopped

1 tablespoon finely chopped fresh mint leaves

¾ cup creamy poppy seed salad dressing

4 SERVINGS

Cook pasta according to package directions; drain in colander and let cool.

Place all ingredients in a large bowl; mix gently to combine. Cover and chill slightly. Serve. Refrigerate leftovers.

Serve with warm soft bakery rolls . . . buttered, of course.

One serving contains approximately: Calories 470, Fat 12g, Carbohydrates 68g, Protein 24g

Curried Chicken Rice Salad

Mix rice, chicken, celery, onions and bell pepper in a large bowl.

Stir together sour cream, mayonnaise, chutney, curry powder, salt, pepper and garlic salt in a small container; add to rice mixture. Mix well. Cover and chill slightly. Serve. Refrigerate leftovers.

Garnish each serving with yellow grape tomatoes.

One serving contains approximately: Calories 392, Fat 20g, Carbohydrates 34g, Protein 17g

INGREDIENTS

3 cups cooked white rice

2 cups diced cooked chicken

½ cup sliced celery

½ cup sliced green onions

¼ cup diced red bell pepper

1 cup sour cream

¼ cup mayonnaise

3 tablespoons mango chutney

2 teaspoons curry powder

½ teaspoon salt

¼ teaspoon ground black pepper

⅛ teaspoon garlic salt

6 SERVINGS

Curried Chicken Salad

INGREDIENTS

4 cups diced skinless, cooked
   rotisserie chicken

1 cup chopped roasted salted cashews

4 green onions, thinly sliced

2 mangoes, peeled, pitted and cut into
   ½-inch cubes

2 stalks celery, chopped

2 tablespoons fresh lemon juice

½ teaspoon freshly grated lemon zest

¼ cup mayonnaise

¼ cup plain yogurt

1½ teaspoons curry powder

½ teaspoon ground cumin

¼ teaspoon ground black pepper

Lettuce leaves

Fresh cilantro

6 SERVINGS

Mix chicken, cashews, green onions, mangoes, celery, lemon juice and lemon zest in a large bowl.

Stir mayonnaise, yogurt, curry powder, cumin and black pepper in a small container until blended. Add to chicken mixture and stir well.

Serve over lettuce leaves; garnish with cilantro. Refrigerate leftovers.

This delicious meal is full of fresh mangoes and roasted cashews.

One serving contains approximately: Calories 475, Fat 31g, Carbohydrates 21g, Protein 31g

Favorite Chicken Pasta Salad

Cook pasta according to package directions; drain and rinse with cold water in a colander, then drain again. Place in a large bowl.

Add all remaining ingredients to bowl. Gently stir to combine. Cover and chill slightly. Serve. Refrigerate leftovers.

Serve over a bed of shredded lettuce along with warm garlic bread.

One serving contains approximately: Calories 262, Fat 3g, Carbohydrates 38g, Protein 18g

INGREDIENTS

1 7-ounce package uncooked dry spiral pasta

1½ 15-ounce cans black beans, rinsed and drained

2 cups diced cooked chicken breast

2 large ripe tomatoes, seeded and chopped

½ cup Italian salad dressing, or to taste

6–8 SERVINGS

Fruited Chicken and Rice Salad

INGREDIENTS

5 cups cubed cooked skinless rotisserie chicken

3 cups cooked rice, cooled

1½ cups diced green bell pepper

1½ cups sliced celery

1 20-ounce can pineapple tidbits, well drained

¾ cup mayonnaise

4 teaspoons fresh orange juice

2 teaspoons white vinegar

1 teaspoon salt

½ teaspoon ground ginger

⅛ teaspoon garlic powder

1 15-ounce can Mandarin oranges, well drained

1 cup toasted slivered almonds

6 SERVINGS

Mix chicken, rice, green bell pepper, celery and pineapple in a large bowl.

Mix mayonnaise, orange juice, vinegar, salt, ginger and garlic powder in a small bowl. Pour over chicken mixture; toss. Cover and chill slightly.

Stir in the oranges and almonds just before serving. Refrigerate leftovers.

Serve this crunchy, fruit-filled almond and rice salad with assorted crackers.

One serving contains approximately: Calories 722, Fat 40g, Carbohydrates 50g, Protein 40g

Greek Chicken Salad

Mix yogurt, mayonnaise, oregano and garlic in a large bowl until creamy. Add chicken, cucumber, tomatoes, feta, parsley and olives; toss. Chill slightly. Serve over salad greens. Refrigerate leftovers.

Serve this quick meal with warm pita bread.

One serving contains approximately: Calories 320, Fat 20g, Carbohydrates 5g, Protein 26g

INGREDIENTS

¾ cup plain yogurt

½ cup mayonnaise

1 teaspoon fresh oregano

3 cloves fresh garlic, finely chopped

3 cups shredded cooked rotisserie chicken breast

1 cup seedless diced cucumber

1 cup cherry tomatoes, halved

½ cup crumbled feta cheese

¼ cup chopped fresh flat-leaf parsley

2 tablespoons chopped pitted kalamata olives

Mixed salad greens

6 SERVINGS

Grilled Chicken Caesar Salad

INGREDIENTS

8 cups torn romaine lettuce

1 pound boneless skinless chicken breasts, grilled and cut into strips

1 cup seasoned croutons

¼ cup shredded Parmesan cheese

½ cup fat-free Caesar Italian salad dressing

4 SERVINGS

Place lettuce, chicken, croutons and cheese in a large bowl; toss.

Add salad dressing just before serving. Refrigerate leftovers.

Serve with warm French garlic bread.

Variation: Use classic Caesar salad dressing. Add crumbled bacon bits.

One serving contains approximately: Calories 260, Fat 7g, Carbohydrates 38g, Protein 15g

Grilled Chicken Salad with Goat Cheese

Spray the grill grate with nonstick cooking spray and preheat to medium-high.

Season chicken with salt and pepper. Grill until cooked through, about 6 minutes per side. Remove from grill; slice into strips.

Whisk vinegar, olive oil, sugar, salt and pepper in a large salad bowl. Add salad greens; toss to coat.

Place equal amounts of salad greens on 4 plates. Top each equally with chicken, raisins and cheese. Serve. Refrigerate leftovers.

Variation: Broil instead of grill. Serve with warm hard rolls.

One serving contains approximately: Calories 406, Fat 14g, Carbohydrates 26g, Protein 45g

INGREDIENTS

Nonstick cooking spray

4 boneless skinless chicken breasts, about 4 ounces each

Salt and black pepper to taste

¼ cup raspberry vinegar

2 tablespoons extra virgin olive oil

½ teaspoon granulated sugar

¼ teaspoon salt

¼ teaspoon ground black pepper

8 cups mixed baby salad greens

½ cup golden raisins

4 tablespoons goat cheese

1 cup fresh raspberries

4 SERVINGS

Grilled Chicken Slaw Salad

INGREDIENTS

1 16-ounce package coleslaw mix

¼ cup light Asian sesame ginger vinaigrette salad dressing, divided

1 pound skinless, boneless chicken breast halves, grilled and thinly sliced

½ cup chow mein noodles

2 green onions, chopped

4 SERVINGS

Mix coleslaw mix, ½ cup salad dressing and grilled chicken in a large bowl.

Sprinkle with noodles and green onions, then drizzle top with remaining salad dressing. Serve immediately. Refrigerate leftovers.

Garnish with fresh melon wedges. Serve with hard rolls.

One serving contains approximately: Calories 300, Fat 11g, Carbohydrates 20g, Protein 29g

Hawaiian Chicken Salad

Mix chicken, salad dressing, macadamia nuts, bell pepper and onions in a large bowl. Cover and chill slightly.

Stir in pineapple just before serving. (For best results, serve salad within one hour after making, because salads with fresh pineapple do not hold well.) Serve immediately over salad greens. Refrigerate leftovers.

Serve with fresh bakery rolls.

One serving contains approximately: Calories 450, Fat 35g, Carbohydrates 16g, Protein 21g

INGREDIENTS

2 cups diced cooked cold rotisserie chicken breast

½ cup key lime salad dressing

½ cup coarsely chopped macadamia nuts

¼ cup chopped red bell pepper

¼ cup sliced green onions

2 cups diced fresh pineapple

Mixed salad greens

4 SERVINGS

Jerk Chicken Salad

INGREDIENTS

2½ cups sliced cooked rotisserie chicken breast

1 teaspoon jerk seasoning, divided

1½ cups shredded Cheddar Jack cheese

1 cup thinly cut carrot strips

½ cup diced cucumber

1 green onion, thinly sliced

¼ cup toasted sliced almonds

¼ cup light mayonnaise

2 tablespoons cider vinegar

Mixed salad greens

4 SERVINGS

Mix chicken and ½ teaspoon jerk seasoning in a medium bowl. Add cheese, carrots, cucumber, onion and almonds.

Mix mayonnaise, vinegar and ½ teaspoon jerk seasoning in a small container; add to chicken mixture; toss. Serve immediately over mixed greens. Refrigerate leftovers.

Garnish with wedges of fresh watermelon and serve with crusty rolls.

Variation: Use a 10-ounce package of cooked chicken breast strips.

One serving contains approximately: Calories 408, Fat 26g, Carbohydrates 9g, Protein 33g

Leafy Chicken Avocado Salad

Gently toss all ingredients except tortilla chips and sliced tomatoes in a large bowl. Place equal amounts of salad mixture on 4 plates. Garnish with sliced tomatoes and top with tortilla chips. Serve immediately. Refrigerate leftovers.

Cooked rotisserie chicken from the market is used in this tasty salad.

One serving contains approximately: Calories 743, Fat 39g, Carbohydrates 44g, Protein 56g

INGREDIENTS

1 large bunch red leaf lettuce, chopped

2 cups fresh corn kernels or drained whole kernel canned corn

1 15-ounce can black beans, rinsed

4 radishes, thinly sliced

½ cup shredded Monterey Jack cheese

6 tablespoons cilantro-lime salad dressing

1 large cooked rotisserie chicken, bones and skin discarded, meat cubed

1 large ripe avocado, peeled, pitted and cubed

½ cup coarsely crushed tortilla chips

1 large ripe tomato, seeded and sliced

4 SERVINGS

Lentil Chicken Salad

INGREDIENTS

1 cup diced cooked chicken

1 cup canned lentils, rinsed under hot
    water and drained in a colander

2 cups shredded iceberg lettuce

1 cup diced celery

½ cup shredded carrot

½ cup chopped pecans

¾ cup mayonnaise

¼ cup chunky salsa

4 green onions, chopped

1 tablespoon chopped fresh
    flat-leaf parsley

1 tablespoon fresh lemon juice

¼ teaspoon ground black pepper

Salt to taste

4 SERVINGS

Mix together chicken, lentils, lettuce, celery, carrot and pecans in a large bowl.

Stir remaining ingredients in a small bowl. Pour mixture over chicken mixture; stir gently to combine. Serve immediately. Refrigerate leftovers.

Garnish each serving with sliced fresh cantaloupe.

One serving contains approximately: Calories 435, Fat 38g, Carbohydrates 12g, Protein 11g

Parmesan Chicken Salad

Mix salad greens, tomatoes, bell pepper and cucumber in a large bowl. Add salad dressing; toss to coat.

Place equal amounts salad mixture on 4 dinner plates. Top each equally with sliced chicken breast and Parmesan cheese. Serve. Refrigerate leftovers.

Variation: Use sliced grilled chicken breast. Serve salad with warm rolls.

One serving contains approximately: Calories 260, Fat 11g, Carbohydrates 20g, Protein 21g

INGREDIENTS

1 10-ounce package mixed salad greens

1 cup halved cherry tomatoes

1 red bell pepper, cut into short thin strips

½ cup diced fresh seedless cucumber

½ cup light ranch salad dressing

8 ounces thinly sliced cooked skinless rotisserie chicken breast

1 cup shredded Parmesan cheese

4 SERVINGS

Pasta Chicken Salad with Pesto Vinaigrette

INGREDIENTS

1 9-ounce package refrigerated three-cheese tortellini

1 7-ounce container refrigerated pesto with basil

3 tablespoons cider vinegar

½ teaspoon seasoned salt

¼ teaspoon granulated sugar

⅛ teaspoon ground black pepper

2½ cups cooked rotisserie skinless chicken breast, cubed

1½ cups sliced and halved fresh zucchini

½ cup chopped red bell pepper

6 SERVINGS

Prepare pasta according to package directions; rinse in a colander with cold water and drain well.

Mix pesto, vinegar, salt, sugar and black pepper in a large bowl. Add chicken, zucchini, bell pepper and pasta to bowl. Toss to mix well. Serve immediately or refrigerate. Refrigerate leftovers.

Variation: Use sliced fresh seedless cucumber rounds instead of zucchini.

One serving contains approximately: Calories 370, Fat 19g, Carbohydrates 25g, Protein 24g

Quick BBQ'd Chicken Salad

Brush both sides of chicken with barbecue sauce. Place chicken on a preheated grill; grill about 6 minutes per side or until juices run clear. Place on a cutting board; slice and keep warm.

Mix salad greens, tomatoes, ¾ cup cheese, red bell pepper, corn, beans, olives and green onions in a large bowl; place equal amounts of salad mixture on 6 plates. Top each with sliced warm chicken.

Mix ranch salad dressing, chili powder and cumin in a small container; drizzle equally over each salad and sprinkle with remaining cheese. Serve. Refrigerate leftovers.

Serve with warm hard rolls.

One serving contains approximately: Calories 516, Fat 34g, Carbohydrates 30g, Protein 25g

INGREDIENTS

6 boneless skinless chicken breast halves

½ cup barbecue sauce

1 10-ounce package mixed salad greens

2 ripe tomatoes, chopped

1½ cups shredded mild Cheddar cheese, divided

1 red bell pepper, thinly sliced

1 11-ounce can whole kernel corn, drained

½ cup canned black beans, rinsed and drained

1 2.5-ounce sliced black olives, drained

2 green onions, thinly sliced

1 cup ranch salad dressing

1 teaspoon chili powder

¾ teaspoon ground cumin

6 SERVINGS

Quick Chicken Caesar Salad

INGREDIENTS

2 tablespoons mayonnaise

2 tablespoons fresh lemon juice

2 tablespoons grated
  Parmesan cheese

1 teaspoon Dijon mustard

¼ teaspoon salt

¼ teaspoon ground black pepper

6 cups torn romaine lettuce

1 skinless boneless cooked rotisserie
  chicken breast, sliced

½ cup garlic croutons

Shaved Parmesan, optional

Anchovy fillets, optional

2 SERVINGS

Whisk mayonnaise, lemon juice, grated cheese, mustard, salt and pepper in a large bowl until combined.

Add lettuce; toss until coated. Add chicken and croutons; toss. Divide salad equally on 2 plates. Top each with shaved Parmesan cheese and anchovy fillets, if desired. Serve immediately. Refrigerate leftovers.

This is a good salad for two.

One serving contains approximately: Calories 363, Fat 21g, Carbohydrates 14g, Protein 27g

Quinoa Chicken Salad

Bring water to a full boil over high heat in a 2-quart saucepan. Stir in quinoa and bouillon granules. Reduce heat to medium-low. Cover and cook until quinoa is tender, about 15 minutes. Spoon into a large bowl.

Mix all dressing ingredients in a small container until blended.

Add chicken, red onion, bell pepper, olives, parsley, minced garlic and cheese to bowl; mix well. Pour dressing over mixture; stir to combine. Serve immediately. Refrigerate leftovers.

This salad is also delicious when served slightly chilled.

Variation: Use cubed poached chicken breast.

One serving contains approximately: Calories 279, Fat 14g, Carbohydrates 21g, Protein 18g

INGREDIENTS

1 cup uncooked quinoa

2 cups water

4 teaspoons chicken bouillon granules

Dressing

¼ cup extra virgin olive oil

⅔ cup fresh lemon juice

1 tablespoon balsamic vinegar

½ teaspoon salt

2 cooked rotisserie chicken breasts, cut into bite-size pieces

1 large red onion, diced

1 large green bell pepper, diced

½ cup chopped kalamata olives

¼ cup chopped fresh flat-leaf parsley

1 clove fresh garlic, minced

½ cup crumbled feta cheese

8 SERVINGS

Rotisserie Chicken Caesar-Style Salad

INGREDIENTS

5 cups chopped romaine lettuce

3 cups cut-up skinless boneless, cooked rotisserie chicken

1 cup chopped fresh tomatoes

5 tablespoons cholesterol-free mayonnaise

¼ cup finely chopped green onions

1 tablespoon fresh lemon juice

¼ teaspoon ground black pepper

Salt to taste

6 SERVINGS

Mix all ingredients in a large bowl. Serve immediately or cover and chill slightly before serving. Refrigerate leftovers.

Serve with toasted garlic French bread or garlic croutons.

One serving contains approximately: Calories 180, Fat 7g, Carbohydrates 4g, Protein 24g

Sam's Pasta Chicken Salad

Cook pasta according to package directions. Rinse in a colander with cold water; drain well and place in a large bowl.

Add chicken, tomatoes, carrots, bell peppers and beans to bowl; mix. Add salad dressing; toss. Serve salad over crisp lettuce. Refrigerate leftovers.

A pasta meal that's so quick to prepare and, like Sam, unforgettable.

One serving contains approximately: Calories 430, Fat 19g, Carbohydrates 40g, Protein 25g

INGREDIENTS

1 cup uncooked medium pasta shells

1 cup cubed cooked rotisserie chicken breast

1 cup halved cherry tomatoes

½ cup thinly sliced carrots

Half of a green bell pepper, cut into 1-inch strips

½ cup large-diced red bell pepper

1 15-ounce can black beans, rinsed and drained

½ cup Italian salad dressing, or to taste

Lettuce leaves

4 SERVINGS

Shells and Black Beans Chicken Salad

INGREDIENTS

1 cup uncooked medium pasta shells

1 cup cubed cooked skinless rotisserie chicken breast

1 cup ½-inch cubed Monterey Jack cheese

1 carrot, cut into matchstick strips

2 medium-size fresh tomatoes, seeded and cut into bite-size pieces

1 medium green bell pepper, cut into 1-inch strips

1 15-ounce can black beans, drained and rinsed

Salt and ground black pepper to taste

¾ cup Italian salad dressing, or to taste

Lettuce leaves

5 SERVINGS

Cook pasta according to package directions. Rinse in a colander with cold water and drain well. Place into a large bowl.

Add chicken, cheese, carrots, tomatoes, bell pepper and beans to bowl. Season with salt and black pepper to taste. Add half the salad dressing at a time. Toss mixture and taste, adding more if needed. Serve over lettuce.

Serve with warm rolls.

Variation: Use poached chicken.

One serving contains approximately: Calories 430, Fat 19g, Carbohydrates 40g, Protein 25g

Smoked Chicken Salad with Fresh Raspberries

Whisk vinegar, vegetable oil, shallots, honey, mustard, salt and pepper in a medium bowl until well blended. Add 1 cup raspberries to bowl; whisk until berries are completely broken.

Toss chicken with half of the salad dressing mixture in a large bowl.

Line 4 dinner plates equally with salad greens. Arrange equal amounts of chicken over greens. Top each equally with raspberries. Sprinkle each with 1 tablespoon almonds. Drizzle each with remaining salad dressing as desired. Serve. Refrigerate leftovers.

Deli chicken is used in this beautiful salad. Serve with soft rolls.

One serving contains approximately: Calories 457, Fat 30g, Carbohydrates 31g, Protein 18g

INGREDIENTS

⅓ cup red wine vinegar

¼ cup vegetable oil

1 tablespoon minced shallots

1 teaspoon honey

½ cup Dijon mustard

¼ teaspoon salt

¼ teaspoon ground white pepper

3 cups fresh raspberries, divided

12 ounces deli smoked chicken breast, sliced

8 cups mixed salad greens

¼ cup toasted sliced almonds

4 SERVINGS

Spinach Salad with Chicken

INGREDIENTS

2 tablespoons cooking oil

4 boneless skinless chicken breast
halves, seasoned with ¼ teaspoon
salt and ¼ teaspoon ground
black pepper

1 10-ounce package fresh
spinach leaves

Half of a small red onion, thinly sliced

½ cup chunky blue cheese
salad dressing

1 fresh red apple, cored and
coarsely chopped

⅓ cup toasted pecans

4 SERVINGS

Heat oil in a 12-inch nonstick skillet over medium-high heat. Add chicken; cook, turning once, about 12 minutes or until thoroughly cooked. Remove to a cutting board. Cool and slice thinly.

Mix spinach, onion and salad dressing in a large bowl. Place equal portions of salad on 4 plates. Top each with sliced chicken. Garnish each with apple and pecans. Serve. Refrigerate leftovers.

Offer more salad dressing and serve with warm blueberry muffins.

One serving contains approximately: Calories 550, Fat 39g, Carbohydrates 15g, Protein 37g

Sweet and Sour Chicken Salad

Heat oil in a 12-inch nonstick skillet over medium-high heat. Rub chicken tenders with jerk seasoning until coated; place in hot skillet. Cook, stirring occasionally, until chicken is no longer pink in center and juices run clear. Remove from skillet; keep warm.

Mix sweet and sour sauce with brown sugar in a small container; add to same hot skillet; stir and cook over medium heat 1 minute. Stir in water and vinegar. Remove from heat. Stir in lettuce to coat. Place equal amounts of lettuce mixture on 4 dinner plates. Top each equally with bell peppers and orange segments. Serve immediately. Refrigerate leftovers.

Serve this sweet and spicy meal for special times.

One serving contains approximately: Calories 220, Fat 4g, Carbohydrates 25g, Protein 23g

INGREDIENTS

1 tablespoon cooking oil

1 14-ounce package fresh (not frozen) chicken breast tenders

1 tablespoon jerk seasoning

⅓ cup sweet and sour sauce

2 tablespoons brown sugar

2 tablespoons water

1 tablespoon rice vinegar or red wine vinegar

8 cups chopped romaine lettuce

½ cup green bell pepper, chopped

½ cup red bell pepper, chopped

1 11-ounce can Mandarin orange segments, drained

4 SERVINGS

Taco Chicken Salad

INGREDIENTS

2 tablespoons cooking oil

1 pound boneless skinless chicken breasts, cut into small cubes

1 1.25-ounce package taco seasoning, divided

2 tablespoons water

¾ cup sour cream, divided

¼ cup salsa

½ cup finely shredded Mexican cheese blend

6 cups mixed salad greens

4 SERVINGS

Heat oil in a medium-size nonstick skillet over medium-high heat until hot. Add chicken; cook and stir until chicken is browned. Stir in 2 tablespoons taco seasoning, water and 2 tablespoons sour cream; cook and stir until chicken is no longer pink in center. Remove from heat; keep warm.

Mix remaining taco seasoning, remaining sour cream, salsa and cheese in a large bowl. Add salad greens; toss and place equal amounts on 4 plates. Top each equally with warm chicken. Serve. Refrigerate leftovers.

Serve this warm salad with crisp cheese breadsticks.

One serving contains approximately: Calories 359, Fat 21g, Carbohydrates 12g, Protein 20g

Tex-Mex Chicken Salad

Whisk olive oil, lime juice, chili powder, cumin and salt in a large bowl.

Add remaining ingredients except cheese and tortillas to bowl; toss.

Place equal amounts salad mixture into 8 salad bowls. Top each equally with cheese and serve each with 1 tortilla half. Refrigerate leftovers.

Variation: Use canned pinto beans. Top with crushed tortilla chips.

One serving contains approximately: Calories 454, Fat 22g, Carbohydrates 34g, Protein 32g

INGREDIENTS

2 tablespoons extra virgin olive oil

5 tablespoons fresh lime juice

1 teaspoon chili powder

¼ teaspoon ground cumin

¼ teaspoon salt

1 large cooked rotisserie chicken, bones and skin discarded, meat coarsely shredded by hand

1 15-ounce can black beans, drained and rinsed

2 cups cherry tomatoes, halved

1 cup whole kernel corn

½ cup diced red onion

2 tablespoons seeded, diced jalapeño pepper, or to taste

1 ripe avocado, peeled pitted and cubed

4 cups shredded iceberg lettuce

1½ cups shredded Cheddar cheese

4 10-inch flour tortillas, warmed and cut in half

8 SERVINGS

Walnut and Cranberry Chicken Salad

INGREDIENTS

1 10-ounce bag mixed salad greens

1 cup dried cranberries

1 6-ounce package deli oven roasted chicken breast cuts

1 4-ounce package crumbled feta cheese

½ cup walnut pieces, toasted

½ cup tangy tomato bacon salad dressing

4 SERVINGS

Put all ingredients in a large bowl. Mix until combined. Serve immediately. Refrigerate leftovers.

Variation: Cubed, cooked skinless rotisserie chicken breast.

Serve this quick meal with warm whole wheat rolls.

One serving contains approximately: Calories 440, Fat 22g, Carbohydrates 39g, Protein 17g

Warm Cheddar Chicken Salad

Toss salad greens, tomatoes and salad dressing in a large bowl until coated; place equal amounts on 4 plates.

Season chicken with jerk seasoning. Heat oil in a large nonstick skillet over medium heat until hot. Add chicken and garlic; cook 5 minutes per side or until chicken juices run clear and chicken is cooked through. Place cheese over chicken; reduce heat to low. Cover and cook 1 minute.

Remove to a cutting board; cut crosswise into thick slices. Place equal amounts on top of each salad. Serve immediately. Refrigerate leftovers.

Serve with warm bread.

One serving contains approximately: Calories 570, Fat 47g, Carbohydrates 6g, Protein 34g

INGREDIENTS

8 cups mixed salad greens

1 cup cherry tomatoes, halved

⅓ cup ranch salad dressing

2 teaspoons jerk seasoning

4 5-ounce boneless skinless chicken breast halves

2 teaspoons cooking oil

2 cloves fresh garlic, minced

4 slices sliced medium Cheddar cheese, cut diagonally in half

4 SERVINGS

Warm Chicken Cabbage Salad

INGREDIENTS

⅓ cup plus 1 tablespoon vegetable oil, divided

⅓ cup red wine vinegar

½ teaspoon salt

½ teaspoon ground black pepper

12 cups shredded savoy cabbage, or green cabbage

3 cups water

3 packages chicken-flavored ramen noodles with seasoning packets

2 tablespoons all-purpose flour

4 boneless skinless chicken breast halves

6 SERVINGS

Mix ⅓ cup oil, vinegar, salt and pepper in an extra large bowl.

Add shredded cabbage; toss well.

Bring 3 cups water to a boil in a large saucepan. Break noodles as directed on package; add to saucepan and cook, stirring occasionally, for 3 minutes. Stir in 2 of the seasoning packets until dissolved; pour mixture over cabbage and stir until well mixed.

Mix flour and remaining seasoning packet in a shallow dish. Add chicken; coat well then shake off excess flour.

Heat 1 tablespoon oil in a large nonstick skillet over medium heat. Add chicken; cook until thoroughly done and no longer pink in center, about 7 minutes each side. Slice cooked chicken crosswise into ½-inch wide pieces.

Place equal amounts of cabbage-noodle mixture on 6 dinner plates. Top equally with sliced chicken. Serve immediately. Refrigerate leftovers.

Enjoy this crunchy cabbage, soft noodles and warm chicken meal.

One serving contains approximately: Calories 354, Fat 11g, Carbohydrates 41g, Protein 25g

Warm Chicken Cobb Salad

Coat a large nonstick skillet with cooking spray. Heat over medium-high heat. Add chicken. Cook about 5 minutes on each side or until juices run clear and chicken is cooked through. Place on a cutting board; cut into thin slices. Keep warm.

Mix salad greens, tomatoes, avocado and onions in a large bowl; toss with salad dressing. Place equal amounts in 4 salad bowls. Top each equally with chicken, cheese and bacon. Serve. Refrigerate leftovers.

Serve with garlic croutons or toasted sourdough bread.

One serving contains approximately: Calories 270, Fat 28g, Carbohydrates 9g, Protein 38g

INGREDIENTS

Nonstick cooking spray

1½ pounds boneless skinless chicken breast cutlets, seasoned with ¼ teaspoon salt and ¼ teaspoon ground black pepper

8 cups mixed salad greens

1 cup ripe cherry or grape tomatoes, halved

1 small ripe avocado, peeled, pitted and diced

2 green onions, thinly sliced

⅓ cup fat-free Italian salad dressing

2 tablespoons crumbled blue cheese

2 slices bacon, cooked crisp and crumbled

4 SERVINGS

Warm Chicken Rice Salad

INGREDIENTS

1 8.8-ounce package precooked
   brown rice

1 tablespoon cooking oil

1 pound chicken breast tenders, cut
   into bite-size pieces

¼ cup frozen peas, thawed

2 green onions, sliced

¼ cup bottled stir-fry sauce

2 tablespoons toasted sliced almonds

4 SERVINGS

Heat rice in microwave according to package directions.

Heat oil in a large nonstick skillet until hot. Add chicken and peas; stir and cook until chicken is no longer pink and juices run clear, about 5 to 6 minutes, depending on thickness of chicken.

Stir in hot cooked rice, green onions and stir-fry sauce until heated. Sprinkle each serving with almonds when serving. Serve immediately. Refrigerate leftovers.

Serve this warm salad with sliced fresh tomatoes.

One serving contains approximately: Calories 300, Fat 8g, Carbohydrates 24g, Protein 31g

Warm Chicken Sausage Salad

Cook sausage on a preheated stovetop grill pan, turning often, until browned and thoroughly heated, about 6 minutes; set aside.

Heat 2 tablespoons olive oil in a large nonstick skillet over medium-high heat. Add bell peppers and garlic; cook and stir 2 minutes. Stir in chickpeas, tomatoes, olives, salt, black pepper and thyme; cook until thoroughly heated, about 3 minutes. Spoon into a large bowl.

Stir in 2 tablespoons olive oil, the lemon juice and lemon zest. Add sausage pieces and arugula; toss. Serve immediately. Refrigerate leftovers.

A slice of warm crusty bread will complete this hearty meal.

One serving contains approximately: Calories 677, Fat 37g, Carbohydrates 42g, Protein 40g

INGREDIENTS

1½ pounds precooked chicken sausage, cut into 1½-inch pieces

4 tablespoons olive oil, divided

½ cup chopped green bell pepper

½ cup chopped red bell pepper

3 cloves fresh garlic, minced

2 15-ounce cans chickpeas, rinsed and drained

1 cup cherry tomatoes, halved

8 pitted kalamata olives, halved

½ teaspoon salt

½ teaspoon ground black pepper

½ teaspoon dried thyme, crushed

2 tablespoons fresh lemon juice

1 teaspoon fresh lemon zest

4 cups fresh arugula or baby spinach

4 SERVINGS

White Beans and Chicken Salad

INGREDIENTS

2 cups cubed skinless cooked
rotisserie chicken breast

1 cup chopped fresh tomatoes

Half of a small red onion, thinly sliced

2 16-ounce cans cannellini beans or
navy beans, rinsed and drained

¼ cup red wine vinegar

2 tablespoons extra virgin olive oil

1 tablespoon fresh lemon juice

2 teaspoons Dijon mustard

½ teaspoon salt

¼ teaspoon ground black pepper

2 cloves fresh garlic, minced

¼ cup chopped fresh basil

4–5 SERVINGS

Put chicken, tomatoes, red onion and beans in a large bowl; toss.

Whisk all remaining ingredients except basil in a small bowl.

Drizzle dressing over salad; toss to coat. Sprinkle each serving with chopped basil. Serve immediately. Refrigerate leftovers.

Serve this hearty meal with warm Italian bread.

One serving contains approximately: Calories 369, Fat 11g, Carbohydrates 42g, Protein 29g

Wild Mushrooms and Chicken Salad

Heat 1 tablespoon oil in a large nonstick skillet over medium heat. Cook chicken about 4 minutes on each side or until tender and juices run clear. Remove chicken from skillet to a cutting board. Slice on an angle lengthwise; cover with foil and keep warm.

Add remaining oil and the butter to same skillet. Add mushrooms; cook and stir until tender, about 3 minutes. Add shallot; cook and stir 1 minute.

Wash and dry salad greens; tear into bite-size pieces and place in a large bowl. Add cooked mushroom mixture.

Whisk mustard, vinegar and olive oil in a small container. Pour over salad mixture in bowl; toss. Place equal amounts salad mixture on 4 plates. Top equally with sliced chicken. Serve immediately. Refrigerate leftovers.

Serve with warm bread.

One serving contains approximately: Calories 333, Fat 36g, Carbohydrates 8g, Protein 13g

INGREDIENTS

2 tablespoons cooking oil, or as needed

2 boneless chicken breast halves, seasoned with salt and black pepper

3 tablespoons butter

1 7-ounce package mixed wild mushrooms, trimmed

1 shallot, finely chopped

6 cups mixed salad greens

2 tablespoons Dijon mustard

2 teaspoons red wine vinegar

⅓ cup extra virgin olive oil

4 SERVINGS

Wilted Spinach Chicken Salad

INGREDIENTS

3 cups boneless skinless cooked rotisserie chicken, coarsely shredded

1 unpeeled Fuji or Red Delicious apple, cored and thinly sliced

1 6-ounce bag baby spinach

3 slices bacon, cut into ½-inch pieces

4 green onions, thinly sliced

⅓ cup cider vinegar

1 tablespoon olive oil

1 tablespoon coarse Dijon mustard

2 tablespoons fresh thyme leaves or ½ teaspoon dried thyme leaves

½ teaspoon salt

¼ teaspoon ground black pepper

4 SERVINGS

Mix chicken, apple and spinach in a large bowl; set aside.

Cook bacon in a medium-size nonstick skillet over medium heat until browned, about 5 minutes. Add green onions to skillet with bacon; stir and cook 1 minute.

Remove skillet from heat. Stir in vinegar, olive oil, mustard, thyme, salt and black pepper. Pour hot mixture over chicken mixture in bowl. Toss to coat. Serve immediately. Refrigerate leftovers.

Rotisserie chicken makes this a simple meal to enjoy. Serve with rolls.

One serving contains approximately: Calories 385, Fat 27g, Carbohydrates 8g, Protein 29g

turkey

Blueberry Turkey Salad

INGREDIENTS

Dressing

½ cup raspberry vinaigrette

¼ teaspoon soy sauce

⅛ teaspoon ground ginger

Salad

6 slices deli white American cheese,
cut into thin strips

1 cup fresh blueberries, rinsed
and drained

⅓ cup sliced green onions

¼ cup thinly sliced celery

¼ cup sliced almonds

1 5-ounce bag spring mix salad greens

1 cup cubed ripe mango

1½ cups oven roasted deli turkey
breast, cut into thin strips

6 SERVINGS

Mix all dressing ingredients in a small container; set aside.

Place all salad ingredients in a large bowl; toss to combine.

Place equal amounts of salad on 6 plates. Drizzle each with salad dressing. Serve. Refrigerate leftovers.

   Variation: Use fresh raspberries. Serve with warm soft rolls.

One serving contains approximately: Calories 260, Fat 19g, Carbohydrates 13g, Protein 11g

Cheese Tortellini Turkey Salad

Cook tortellini according to package directions. Rinse in cold water and drain well. Put pasta in a large bowl. Add turkey, zucchini and bell pepper.

Mix pesto, vinegar, salt, sugar and black pepper in a small container. Add to bowl; toss salad until coated. Serve. Refrigerate leftovers.

Serve with warm Italian bread.

Variation: For extra color, add fresh broccoli pieces and diced fresh carrots to this quick salad.

One serving contains approximately: Calories 370, Fat 19g, Carbohydrates 25g, Protein 24g

INGREDIENTS

1 9-ounce package refrigerated three-cheese tortellini

2½ cups thin strips of cooked turkey

1½ cups sliced and halved fresh zucchini

½ cup seeded, chopped red bell pepper

1 7-ounce container pesto with basil

3 tablespoons cider vinegar

½ teaspoon salt

¼ teaspoon granulated sugar

⅛ teaspoon ground black pepper

6 SERVINGS

Chili Pasta Salad

INGREDIENTS

½ cup uncooked pasta shells

1 15-ounce can turkey chili with beans

1 11-ounce can whole kernel corn with red and green peppers, drained

4 cups shredded romaine lettuce

¼ cup shredded Cheddar cheese

2 green onions, thinly sliced

4 SERVINGS

Cook pasta according to package directions; drain pasta and return to pot.

Add chili and corn. Cook over medium heat until heated.

Line 4 salad bowls equally with lettuce. Top each with 1 cup chili mixture, 1 tablespoon cheese and equal amounts of green onions. Serve immediately. Refrigerate leftovers.

Serve this warm salad with sour cream and corn chips.

One serving contains approximately: Calories 230, Fat 4g, Carbohydrates 38g, Protein 11g

Club Turkey Pasta Salad

Mix all dressing ingredients in a small container; set aside.

Cook pasta according to package directions. Drain, then rinse in cold water; drain well again. Place pasta into a large bowl. Add remaining salad ingredients. Pour dressing over salad just before serving. Toss to coat. Serve. Refrigerate leftovers.

Leftover turkey is perfect for this salad.

One serving contains approximately: Calories 400, Fat 7g, Carbohydrates 28g, Protein 19g

INGREDIENTS

Dressing

¾ cup light mayonnaise

1 teaspoon granulated sugar

⅛ teaspoon ground black pepper

2 tablespoons milk

2 tablespoons white wine vinegar

2 teaspoons Dijon mustard

Salad

6 ounces (2 cups) uncooked radiatore pasta

6 slices bacon, crisply cooked and crumbled

2 cups shredded iceberg lettuce

1½ cups cubed cooked turkey breast

½ cup cubed Colby-Monterey Jack cheese blend

8 cherry tomatoes, quartered

1 ripe avocado, peeled, pitted and cubed

6 SERVINGS

Couscous Turkey Salad

INGREDIENTS

1 10-ounce box plain couscous

¾ pound smoked turkey, diced

1½ cups cherry tomatoes, halved

¼ cup coarsely chopped fresh
   flat-leaf parsley

2 green onions, thinly sliced

½ cup pitted kalamata olives, sliced

½ cup Greek salad dressing

¼ cup toasted slivered almonds

4 SERVINGS

Cook couscous according to package directions; spoon into a large bowl.

Add remaining ingredients to bowl; toss to combine. Serve immediately. Refrigerate leftovers.

Smoked turkey from the deli makes this an easy meal to prepare. Serve over fresh baby spinach leaves.

One serving contains approximately: Calories 554, Fat 4g, Carbohydrates 87g, Protein 23g

Fiesta Turkey Salad

Place lettuce, turkey, bacon and green onions in a large bowl.

Mix mayonnaise and salsa in a small container; add to turkey mixture and toss until well mixed. Serve. Refrigerate leftovers

This is a quick meal to make with that leftover Thanksgiving turkey. Add diced tomatoes, black beans, cheese and green olives for added goodness!

One serving contains approximately: Calories 350, Fat 5g, Carbohydrates 4g, Protein 25g

INGREDIENTS

6 cups torn romaine lettuce

2 cups diced cooked turkey

4 slices bacon, crisply cooked, drained and crumbled

2 green onions, chopped

½ cup mayonnaise

½ cup prepared salsa

4 SERVINGS

Fresh Tomato and Avocado Turkey Salad

INGREDIENTS

Salad

2 large tomatoes, cut into wedges

1 avocado, peeled, pitted and cubed

6 cups green leaf lettuce

½ pound sliced deli turkey

1 small red onion, thinly sliced

2 ounces (½ cup) Parmesan cheese, shaved

Dressing

4 tablespoons extra virgin olive oil

2 tablespoons balsamic vinegar

½ teaspoon salt

¼ teaspoon black pepper

4 SERVINGS

Place all salad ingredients in a large bowl; toss lightly.

Whisk all dressing ingredients in a small container; pour over salad in bowl and toss to coat. Serve. Refrigerate leftovers.

Offer warm rolls when serving this quick salad . . . buttered, of course.

One serving contains approximately: Calories 337, Fat 25g, Carbohydrates 11g, Protein 20g

Provolone Cheese and Smoked Turkey Salad

Place all ingredients except Italian dressing and Parmesan cheese into a large bowl; toss.

Add Italian dressing just before serving; toss.

Place equal amounts of salad into 4 salad bowls. Sprinkle with Parmesan cheese. Serve. Refrigerate leftovers.

This salad is simple and delicious!

One serving contains approximately: Calories 270, Fat 22g, Carbohydrates 8g, Protein 13g

INGREDIENTS

1 5-ounce package mixed salad greens

¼ pound sliced deli smoked provolone cheese cubed into ½-inch pieces

¼ pound sliced deli smoked turkey breast, cut into thin strips

½ cup pitted ripe olives

4 pepperoncini peppers

1 firm-ripe tomato, cut into wedges

2 thin slices red onion, separated into rings

½ cup purchased zesty Italian dressing

Shredded Parmesan cheese

4 SERVINGS

Smoked Turkey Cheese Rice Salad

INGREDIENTS

2½ cups cooked brown rice, chilled

1 pound deli smoked turkey breast,
cut into ½-inch pieces

2 ripe medium-size tomatoes, diced

1 small fresh green bell pepper, diced

½ cup diced red onion

¼ cup chopped fresh cilantro
or flat-leaf parsley

1½ cups shredded pizza double
cheese blend, divided

½ cup ranch salad dressing

Lettuce leaves

6 SERVINGS

Mix all ingredients except ½-cup cheese and lettuce in a large bowl; toss until coated. Line 6 plates with leaf lettuce; spoon each with equal amounts of salad mixture. Sprinkle tops with remaining cheese. Chill slightly. Serve. Refrigerate leftovers.

Cooked brown rice can be found in the freezer section of the food market.

One serving contains approximately: Calories 287, Fat 22g, Carbohydrates 25g, Protein 32g

South of the Border Turkey Salad

Heat oil in a medium nonstick skillet over medium-high heat.

Add turkey, salt, black pepper, chili powder and cumin; stir and cook until no longer pink, about 6 minutes. Drain excess liquid. Stir in half the salsa; cook until thoroughly heated, about 3 minutes. Mix sour cream and remaining salsa in a small container; set aside.

Line 4 salad bowls with equal amount of lettuce. Spoon equal amounts of turkey mixture, beans, avocado, cheese, olives and tortilla chips in each bowl. Top equally with sour cream mixture. Serve. Refrigerate leftovers.

Add chopped onions and cubed fresh tomatoes for extra goodness.

One serving contains approximately: Calories 602, Fat 29g, Carbohydrates 47g, Protein 43g

INGREDIENTS

1 tablespoon cooking oil

1 pound fresh ground turkey

½ teaspoon salt

¼ teaspoon ground black pepper

¼ teaspoon chili powder

¼ teaspoon ground cumin

1 16-ounce container refrigerated fresh salsa, divided

2 tablespoons sour cream

8 cups romaine lettuce cut into small chunks

1 15-ounce can pinto beans, drained

1 avocado, peeled, cored and diced

1 cup grated Cheddar cheese

1 6-ounce can sliced black olives

4 ounces tortilla chips

4 SERVINGS

Turkey Brown Rice Salad

INGREDIENTS

2 cups cubed cooked turkey breast

2 cups cooked brown rice

1 cup seedless red grapes, halved

½ cup diced red bell pepper

½ cup chopped celery

4 green onions, sliced

1 tablespoon chopped fresh
  flat-leaf parsley

½ cup dried cranberries

½ cup coarsely chopped pecans,
  toasted

⅓ cup raspberry vinaigrette

7 SERVINGS

Place all ingredients except vinaigrette in a large bowl; mix well.

Drizzle with vinaigrette; toss until coated. Serve.
Refrigerate leftovers.

Look for cooked rice in the freezer section of the supermarket.

One serving contains approximately: Calories 230, Fat 7, Carbohydrates 28g, Protein 15g

Turkey Cranberry Pasta Salad

Cook pasta according to package directions. Drain, then rinse with cold water until cool, then drain well again. Place in a large bowl. Add turkey, grapes, cranberries and celery; toss lightly.

Stir together sour cream, honey and salt in a small container. Pour mixture over pasta mixture; stir to coat. Sprinkle with almonds just before serving. Refrigerate leftovers.

Serve over a bed of torn butter lettuce.

One serving contains approximately: Calories 577, Fat 12g, Carbohydrates 100g, Protein 18g

INGREDIENTS

3 cups uncooked penne pasta

2 cups diced cooked turkey

1 cup red grapes, halved

½ cup sweetened dried cranberries

½ cup diced celery

¾ cup sour cream

2 tablespoons honey

½ teaspoon salt

½ cup sliced toasted almonds

6 SERVINGS

Turkey Cranberry Pear Salad

INGREDIENTS

4 cups torn romaine lettuce leaves

2 cups baby spinach leaves or mixed salad greens

2 cups diced cooked turkey

½ cup mayonnaise

½ cup whole berry cranberry sauce

1 ripe pear, cored and thinly sliced

¼ cup toasted chopped pecans

¼ cup thinly sliced red onion

Dried cranberries, optional

4 SERVINGS

Mix lettuce, spinach leaves and turkey in a large bowl. Mix mayonnaise and cranberry sauce in a small container; add to bowl and toss to coat.

Serve salad mixture equally on 4 individual plates. Top equally with pear, pecans, onion and dried cranberries. Serve. Refrigerate leftovers.

This is a delicious way to use Thanksgiving leftovers!

One serving contains approximately: Calories 430, Fat 28g, Carbohydrates 23g, Protein 24g

Turkey Pasta Salad

Cook pasta according to package directions. Drain. Rinse with cold water then drain well again. Put cool pasta in a large bowl. Add turkey, celery, onion and red pepper.

Mix next six ingredients in a small container until blended. Pour mixture over pasta mixture; mix well. Sprinkle salad with almonds just before serving. Refrigerate leftovers.

This is a good way to use that leftover turkey. Serve salad over shredded lettuce along with a side of sliced tomatoes and buttered bread.

One serving contains approximately: Calories 380, Fat 24g, Carbohydrates 30g, Protein 11g

INGREDIENTS

2 cups uncooked rotini pasta

1 cup cubed cooked turkey

1 cup chopped celery

¾ cup chopped red onion

1 green bell pepper, seeded and chopped

1 cup sour cream

1 cup salad dressing

1 teaspoon garlic salt

1 teaspoon paprika , or to taste

¼ teaspoon ground black pepper

1 1-ounce package ranch salad dressing

½ cup toasted slivered almonds

6 SERVINGS

Turkey Rice Salad

INGREDIENTS

1¾ cups cold water

2¼ cups quick-cooking brown rice

1¾ cups finely chopped cooked turkey

1 cup diced apples

1 cup chopped sweet red peppers

½ cup chopped celery

2 tablespoons currants or
   golden raisins

⅓ cup fresh lemon juice

⅓ cup apple juice

2 tablespoons extra virgin olive oil

Salt and ground black pepper to taste

2 tablespoons toasted slivered
   almonds, or broken walnut pieces

8 SERVINGS

Bring water to a boil in a 2-quart saucepan over high heat. Stir in rice. Reduce heat to medium. Cover and simmer 5 minutes. Remove saucepan from heat; let stand 5 minutes or until all liquid is absorbed. Fluff rice with a fork and place in a large bowl.

Add turkey, apples, peppers, celery and currants to bowl.

Whisk lemon juice, apple juice and olive oil in a small container. Pour mixture over turkey mixture. Season with salt and black pepper to taste. Toss to mix well. Sprinkle with almonds. Serve. Refrigerate leftovers.

Use your leftover turkey for this quick salad or purchase cooked turkey from the deli. Serve with warm rolls.

One serving contains approximately: Calories 258, Fat 13, Carbohydrates 52g, Protein 13g

Turkey Taco Salad

Heat oil over medium-high heat in a nonstick medium-size skillet. Add onion; stir and cook until soft, about 2 minutes. Add turkey and garlic; stir and cook until no trace of pink remains, about 8 minutes. Stir in chili powder, ground cumin, salt and pepper.

Place equal amounts of lettuce in 4 salad bowls; top each with equal amounts of turkey mixture, tortilla chips, cheese and avocado. Top with equal amounts of salsa. Serve. Refrigerate leftovers.

Ground turkey is used in this quick taco salad.

One serving contains approximately: Calories 722, Fat 13g, Carbohydrates 47g, Protein 35g

INGREDIENTS

1 tablespoon cooking oil

½ cup chopped onion

1 pound ground turkey

1 small clove garlic, chopped

½ teaspoon chili powder

¼ teaspoon ground cumin

½ teaspoon salt

¼ teaspoon black pepper

2 heads romaine lettuce, torn

8 ounces tortilla chips

1 cup sliced Cheddar cheese (4 ounces)

1 avocado, peeled, pitted and diced

1 cup purchased fresh salsa

4 SERVINGS

Waldorf Turkey Salad

INGREDIENTS

2 medium Red Delicious apples cut into small cubes

½ cup chopped celery

1½ cups cubed smoked turkey

⅓ cup reduced-calorie mayonnaise

4 cups torn bibb lettuce

¼ cup toasted chopped walnuts

4 SERVINGS

Mix first 4 ingredients in a medium-size bowl; toss lightly until coated.

Place 1 cup lettuce in each of 4 salad bowls; top with equal amounts of salad mixture. Sprinkle equally with walnuts. Serve. Refrigerate leftovers.

Apples and walnuts are found in this delicious salad.

One serving contains approximately: Calories 230, Fat 13g, Carbohydrates 15g, Protein 12g

Zesty Turkey Rice Salad

Mix turkey, rice, peas, carrots, onion and chives in a large bowl.

Mix all dressing ingredients in a small container. Pour over turkey mixture; mix well. Cover and chill slightly. Serve. Refrigerate leftovers.

Garnish with fresh sliced tomatoes. Serve with warm rolls.

One serving contains approximately: Calories 430, Fat 18g, Carbohydrates 33g, Protein 32g

INGREDIENTS

1½ cups cubed cooked turkey

½ cup cooked white rice, cooled

⅔ cup cooked petite sweet peas, cooled

¼ cup diced fresh carrots

2 tablespoons chopped red onion

1 tablespoon chopped fresh chives

Dressing

5 tablespoons sour cream

1 tablespoon cooking oil

1 tablespoon fresh lemon juice

1 tablespoon chutney

½ teaspoon curry powder

¼ teaspoon salt

⅛ teaspoon ground black pepper

2 SERVINGS

seafood

Ali's Salmon Salad

Place lettuce and salad dressing in a large bowl; toss to mix well. Gently fold in salmon and Parmesan cheese. Top each serving with croutons. Serve immediately. Refrigerate leftovers.

Garnish this quick meal with sliced tomatoes. Serve with warm rolls.

One serving contains approximately: Calories 364, Fat 25g, Carbohydrates 15g, Protein 21g

INGREDIENTS

5 cups coarsely chopped romaine lettuce

¾ cup Caesar salad dressing

2 6-ounce cans pink salmon, drained and broken into small chunks

½ cup grated Parmesan cheese

2 cups seasoned croutons

4 SERVINGS

Asian Fish Salad

INGREDIENTS

1 pound tilapia, cut into 1½-inch strips

2 scallions, chopped

¼ cup sesame ginger dressing, divided

1 15-ounce can sliced baby corn, drained and rinsed

1 10-ounce bag mixed salad greens

4 SERVINGS

Combine fish, scallions and 2 tablespoons dressing in a medium bowl; let marinate 5 minutes in the refrigerator.

Heat broiler. Place fish on a foil-lined baking sheet. Broil for about 7 minutes or until fish is cooked through.

Toss remaining salad dressing, baby corn and salad greens in a large bowl until coated. Place equal amounts of salad and fish in 4 salad bowls. Serve. Refrigerate leftovers.

For a summer supper, serve with assorted crackers and iced tea.

One serving contains approximately: Calories 230, Fat 7g, Carbohydrates 12g, Protein 30g

Avocado Crab Salad

Place all ingredients except salad greens in large bowl; mix well.

Serve salad mixture over salad greens. Refrigerate leftovers.

Serve this light meal with favorite crackers or breadsticks.

One serving contains approximately: Calories 288, Fat 18g, Carbohydrates 21g, Protein 18g

1 6-ounce can crabmeat, drained

1 ripe avocado, peeled, pitted and cubed

1 tablespoon low-fat yogurt

½ tablespoon mayonnaise

2 tablespoons fresh lime juice

2 ripe tomatoes, chopped

1 small cucumber, sliced

½ cup chopped fresh cilantro

1 tablespoon chopped red onion

¼ teaspoon cayenne pepper, or to taste

⅛ teaspoon salt, or to taste

⅛ teaspoon ground black pepper

2 cups mixed salad greens

2 SERVINGS

Bacon and Shrimp Pasta Salad

INGREDIENTS

12 ounces uncooked rotini pasta

4 slices bacon, cut into bite-size pieces

1 pound fresh large shrimp, peeled and deveined, tails removed

½ cup water

½ cup fresh basil leaves, chopped

¼ cup fresh lemon juice

½ teaspoon fresh lemon zest

4 SERVINGS

Cook pasta according to package directions. Drain pasta and keep warm.

Cook bacon in a large nonstick skillet over medium heat until crisp. Remove bacon from skillet and place on paper towels to drain well. Leave 1 tablespoon bacon drippings in skillet.

Cut shrimp in half crosswise; add to skillet. Stir and cook over medium heat 4 minutes. Add water; bring to a boil and continue cooking over medium heat 2 minutes. Remove skillet from heat. Stir in basil, lemon juice and lemon zest. Add bacon and pasta; toss. Serve. Refrigerate leftovers.

My brother Nelan ran a seafood business in Eunice, Louisiana. Shrimp was always a favorite meal . . . of course, he would have Tabasco handy!

One serving contains approximately: Calories 505, Fat 10g, Carbohydrates 66g, Protein 36g

Bow Tie Salmon Salad

Cook pasta according to package directions; drain well and cool. Place in a large bowl. Stir in salmon, asparagus, bell pepper and green onions.

Whisk olive oil, lemon juice, dill, salt, black pepper and pepper flakes in a small container. Pour over pasta mixture; mix well. Cover and chill slightly. Serve. Refrigerate leftovers.

Smoked salmon is used in this tasty salad.

One serving contains approximately: Calories 378, Fat 17g, Carbohydrates 41g, Protein 17g

INGREDIENTS

8 ounces uncooked bow tie pasta

8 ounces smoked salmon, broken into bite-size pieces

12 ounces blanched tender asparagus, cooled, and cut into 2-inch pieces

½ cup diced red bell pepper

¼ cup sliced green onions

⅓ cup extra virgin olive oil

¼ cup fresh lemon juice

¼ cup chopped fresh dill

1 teaspoon sea salt, or to taste

½ teaspoon ground black pepper

¼ teaspoon crushed red pepper flakes

4 SERVINGS

Broiled Fish Salad

INGREDIENTS

Salsa

4 ounces crushed pineapple in juice, drained, 1 tablespoon juice reserved

1 cup fresh strawberries, stems removed, halved

¼ cup diced fresh cucumber

2 tablespoons chopped fresh mint leaves or parsley

1 tablespoon wine vinegar

1 tablespoon thinly sliced green onion

2 5-ounce tilapia fillets, thawed and patted dry if frozen

Cooking spray

¼ teaspoon seasoned salt

¼ teaspoon paprika

2 cups loosely packed fresh spinach

2 SERVINGS

Mix all salsa ingredients in a bowl; set aside.

Set oven control to broil. Place fish on rack in broiler pan. Spray tops of fish with cooking spray. Sprinkle tops with reserved 1 tablespoon pineapple juice, salt, and paprika. Broil about 4 to 6 inches from heat, for about 6 to 8 minutes or until fish flakes easily with a fork.

Place equal amount of spinach on each plate. Top each with warm fish. Spoon salsa over all. Serve. Refrigerate leftovers.

Other mild-flavored fish will work fine for this salad.

One serving contains approximately: Calories 210, Fat 3g, Carbohydrates 17g, Protein 28g

Broiled Salmon Salad

Mix mayonnaise, onion, cilantro and lime juice in a small container; reserve ½ cup dressing.

Broil salmon, turning once, and brushing with remaining dressing, until salmon flakes with a fork.

Stir tomato into reserved ½ cup dressing.

Line individual plates with equal amounts of lettuce. Add salmon to each and top equally with dressing. Serve. Refrigerate leftovers.

A refreshing lime dressing tops this seafood salad.

One serving contains approximately: Calories 440, Fat 4.5g, Carbohydrates 4g, Protein 35g

INGREDIENTS

Dressing

½ cup mayonnaise

¼ cup chopped red onion

2 tablespoons chopped fresh cilantro or flat-leaf parsley

1 tablespoons fresh lime juice

4 salmon fillets or salmon steaks (l½ pounds total)

1 tomato, chopped

1 large head romaine or green leaf lettuce, torn

4 SERVINGS

Cabbage and Crab Salad

INGREDIENTS

2½ cups shredded green cabbage

1 cup shredded red cabbage

1 head fresh broccoli, cut into florets

1 green bell pepper, thinly sliced

1 red bell pepper, thinly sliced

1 pound imitation crabmeat, coarsely chopped

¾ cup mayonnaise

¼ cup fresh lemon juice

2 tablespoons granulated sugar

3 tablespoons white wine vinegar

1 clove garlic, crushed

1½ teaspoons Worcestershire sauce

½ teaspoon salt

½ teaspoon ground black pepper

½ teaspoon Tabasco sauce

8 SERVINGS

Mix first six ingredients in a large bowl.

Whisk remaining ingredients in a small bowl until well blended; add to bowl with cabbage. Mix well. Chill slightly and serve. Refrigerate leftovers.

Imitation crabmeat is used in this tasty salad. Serve with hard rolls.

One serving contains approximately: Calories 230, Fat 4g, Carbohydrates 38g, Protein 11g

California Roll Salad

Prepare rice according to package directions. Place rice in a medium bowl; toss with 1 tablespoon vinegar.

Place lettuce leaves on a large serving platter. Top with rice mixture, cucumber, avocado and crabmeat.

Mix soy sauce and 2 tablespoons vinegar in a small container. Drizzle evenly over salad on platter. Sprinkle top evenly with ginger. Serve immediately. Refrigerate leftovers.

This quick salad will please the gourmet in your family! Use imitation crabmeat, if desired. Serve with toasted baguette slices.

One serving contains approximately: Calories 310, Fat 9g, Carbohydrates 42g, Protein 18g

INGREDIENTS

1 8-ounce package precooked white rice in microwavable cups

3 tablespoons seasoned light rice vinegar, divided

1 head Boston lettuce

1 seedless cucumber, unpeeled, thinly sliced

1 ripe avocado, peeled, pitted and sliced

1 pound pasteurized lump crabmeat, picked over for shells

3 tablespoons soy sauce

2 tablespoons slivered pickled ginger

4 SERVINGS

Cool Shrimp Caesar Salad

INGREDIENTS

1 pound cooked shrimp

1 10-ounce bag torn romaine lettuce

1 ripe avocado, peeled, pitted
  and cubed

¾ cup Caesar salad dressing

1 cup broken chili and lime
  tortilla chips

Grated Parmesan cheese, optional

4 SERVINGS

Mix shrimp, lettuce, avocado and salad dressing in a large bowl. Serve on 4 individual dinner plates. Sprinkle each with taco chips. Top with Parmesan cheese if desired. Serve. Refrigerate leftovers.

Variation: Top salad with croutons instead of taco chips, if preferred. Garnish each serving with fresh tomato wedges and sliced hard-boiled egg.

One serving contains approximately: Calories 280, Fat 11g, Carbohydrates 4g, Protein 27g

Couscous Shrimp Salad

Bring water to a boil in a 2-quart saucepan. Stir in couscous. Remove saucepan from heat; cover and let stand 5 minutes. Place couscous in a large bowl and fluff with a fork; cool.

Dressing: Whisk olive oil, vinegar, mustard, cumin, salt, black pepper and garlic in a small container until blended.

Add shrimp, bell peppers, onion, tomatoes, parsley and cheese to cooled couscous in bowl; mix well.

Stir half the salad dressing at a time into the couscous mixture, adding more, if needed, to coat well. Chill slightly. Serve. Refrigerate leftovers.

Serve this delicious salad over lettuce leaves.

One serving contains approximately: Calories 530, Fat 29g, Carbohydrates 39g, Protein 28g

INGREDIENTS

2 cups water

2 cups plain uncooked couscous

Dressing

¾ cup extra virgin olive oil

¼ cup apple cider vinegar

1 teaspoon Dijon mustard

1 teaspoon ground cumin

¼ teaspoon salt, or to taste

¼ teaspoon ground black pepper

2 cloves fresh garlic, crushed

1½ pounds cooked shrimp, peeled and deveined

1 cup chopped red bell pepper

1 cup chopped yellow bell pepper

¼ cup chopped red onion

2 ripe tomatoes, chopped

¾ cup chopped fresh flat-leaf parsley

1 cup crumbled feta cheese

8 SERVINGS

Crab Pasta Salad for Two

INGREDIENTS

8 ounces uncooked spiral or
  penne pasta

⅓ cup prepared pesto sauce

1 6-ounce can lump crabmeat

⅔ cup diced roma tomatoes or halved
  grape tomatoes

2 tablespoons chopped fresh basil

Grated Parmesan cheese, optional

2 SERVINGS

Cook pasta according to package directions. Drain and place in a large bowl; toss with pesto sauce and place equal amounts on 2 dinner plates. Top each equally with crabmeat and tomatoes.

Sprinkle with chopped basil and Parmesan cheese, if desired. Serve immediately. Refrigerate leftovers.

Serve this pretty salad over leaf lettuce. Serve with warm hard rolls.

One serving contains approximately: Calories 822, Fat 49g, Carbohydrates 64g, Protein 33g

Creamy Shrimp Salad

Mix all dressing ingredients in a large bowl until blended.

Add remaining ingredients to bowl; toss. Serve. Refrigerate leftovers.

Cornichons (small pickles) add a tangy flavor to this quick salad.

One serving contains approximately: Calories 216, Fat 5g, Carbohydrates 13g, Protein 28g

INGREDIENTS

Dressing

¼ **cup buttermilk**

¼ **cup sour cream**

½ **cup cornichons, sliced, plus 3 tablespoons of brine from the pickles**

¼ **teaspoon salt**

¼ **teaspoon freshly ground black pepper**

1 **pound cooked peeled and deveined medium-size shrimp**

6 **cups torn Boston lettuce**

2 **heads endive, sliced**

1 **English cucumber, thinly sliced**

6 **radishes, sliced**

2 **tablespoons chopped fresh tarragon or flat-leaf parsley**

4 SERVINGS

Crunchy Tuna Salad

INGREDIENTS

3 12-ounce cans water-packed tuna,
   drained

1 8-ounce can sliced water chestnuts,
   drained

1 2-ounce jar diced pimentos, drained
   and chopped

1½ cups chopped cashews

¾ cup chopped green onions

½ cup sliced celery

¼ cup chopped green bell pepper

1½ cups mayonnaise

1 tablespoon cider vinegar or red
   wine vinegar

½ teaspoon salt

¼ teaspoon ground black pepper

3 cups chow mein noodles

6 SERVINGS

Flake drained tuna in a large bowl.

Mix remaining ingredients except chow mein noodles in another bowl; spoon mixture over tuna and gently toss to combine. Serve over chow mein noodles. Refrigerate leftovers.

Garnish each serving with halved cherry tomatoes.

One serving contains approximately: Calories 814, Fat 68g, Carbohydrates 26g, Protein 22g

Curried Shrimp Rice Salad

Mix all dressing ingredients in a small container until blended.

Place remaining ingredient in a large bowl; add dressing and gently toss until coated. Cover and chill slightly. Serve. Refrigerate leftovers.

Look for cooked rice in the freezer section of your food market. Serve with crusty hard rolls, and garnish each serving with sliced fresh tomatoes.

One serving contains approximately: Calories 310, Fat 15g, Carbohydrates 27g, Protein 16g

INGREDIENTS

Dressing

½ cup corn oil

3 tablespoons cider vinegar or fresh lemon juice

1 tablespoon brown sugar

1 tablespoon soy sauce

2 teaspoons curry powder

½ teaspoon salt

¼ teaspoon ground black pepper

3 cups cooked white rice

1 pound peeled and cooked medium-size shrimp, halved crosswise

1 cup frozen petite peas, thawed

1½ cups chopped celery

½ cup chopped yellow onion

8 SERVINGS

Dilled Tuna Pasta Salad

INGREDIENTS

1 7-ounce package small shell pasta

1 6-ounce can tuna, drained

¼ cup chopped yellow onion

¼ cup chopped green bell pepper

¼ cup chopped celery

¾ cup mayonnaise

¼ cup whole milk

1 tablespoon fresh lemon juice

2 teaspoons prepared yellow mustard

1 teaspoon dill weed

½ teaspoon salt

¼ teaspoon ground black pepper

4 SERVINGS

Cook pasta according to package directions; drain in a colander and rinse with cold water then drain again. Place in a large bowl. Add tuna, onion, bell pepper and celery; mix well.

Mix remaining ingredients in a small container until blended. Add to pasta mixture; toss to coat well. Cover and chill slightly before serving. Refrigerate leftovers.

Garnish with pickles and tomato wedges. Serve with cheese breadsticks.

One serving contains approximately: Calories 230, Fat 4g, Carbohydrates 38g, Protein 11g

Fresh Salmon Pasta Salad

Cook pasta according to package directions. Drain. Rinse with cold water until cold and drain well again. Place in a large bowl. Add salmon, tomatoes, cucumber and onion.

Whisk oil, lemon juice, dill, garlic, salt and pepper in a small bowl; pour over pasta mixture in bowl and gently mix until coated. Chill slightly. Serve over lettuce. Refrigerate leftovers.

Enjoy this salad with fresh salmon or use pink canned salmon instead.

One serving contains approximately: Calories 332, Fat 18, Carbohydrates 27g, Protein 16g

INGREDIENTS

1 8-ounce package uncooked spiral pasta

2 cups fully cooked fresh salmon

1½ cups quartered cherry tomatoes, or thinly sliced roma tomatoes

1 cucumber, halved lengthwise then sliced

1 small red onion, thinly sliced

½ cup vegetable oil

⅓ cup fresh lemon juice

1½ teaspoons dried dill weed or 2 tablespoons fresh dill, minced

2 small garlic cloves, minced

¾ teaspoon salt

¼ teaspoon ground black pepper

Torn iceberg lettuce

6–8 SERVINGS

Fresh Salmon Salad

INGREDIENTS

4 5-ounce fresh salmon steaks

7 tablespoons olive oil, divided

3 tablespoons red wine vinegar
or cider vinegar

1 teaspoon Dijon mustard

¼ teaspoon salt, or to taste

¼ teaspoon ground black pepper

1 large fennel bulb, trimmed,
thinly sliced

4 large firm, ripe tomatoes, cut
into wedges

½ cup frozen edamame, blanched,
drained and cooled

¼ cup capers

Fresh dill

4 SERVINGS

Brush both sides of steaks with 2 tablespoons olive oil and place in a preheated large heavy nonstick skillet. Cook uncovered over medium-high heat, shaking skillet occasionally to keep from sticking, until browned, about 4 minutes. Reduce heat. Turn steaks over and cover skillet tightly. Cook until salmon is opaque throughout, about 4 minutes. Remove from skillet; cool.

Whisk remaining olive oil, vinegar, mustard, salt and pepper in a large bowl. Add fennel, tomatoes, edamame and capers; toss.

Discard skin from steaks. Break salmon into large chunks. Add to salad in bowl; gently toss to coat. Serve. Top each serving with snipped fresh dill as desired. Refrigerate leftovers.

Use frozen salmon, thawed, if fresh salmon is not readily available.

One serving contains approximately: Calories 468, Fat 31g, Carbohydrates 15g, Protein 34g

Greek Shrimp Pasta Salad

Bring 6 cups water to a boil in a large saucepan. Add shrimp; cook about 3 minutes or until done. Remove from saucepan. Peel and devein shrimp; remove tails. Place in a large bowl; cool.

Add remaining ingredients except feta cheese, black pepper and parsley to bowl with shrimp; toss gently to coat. Cover and chill slightly. Sprinkle with feta cheese, black pepper and parsley. Serve. Refrigerate leftovers.

Variation: Use precooked shrimp. Serve with warm rolls.

One serving contains approximately: Calories 344, Fat 11g, Carbohydrates 40g, Protein 20g

INGREDIENTS

1 pound large fresh shrimp

½ cup low-fat Caesar salad dressing

2 teaspoons sun-dried tomato sprinkles

¾ teaspoon dried rosemary, crushed

5 cups cooked penne pasta, cooled

¾ cup thinly sliced cucumber

⅓ cup chopped fresh basil

¼ cup chopped pitted kalamata olives

¼ cup sliced red onion, separated into rings

1 7-ounce bottle roasted red bell peppers, drained and cut into strips

3 ounces crumbled feta cheese

¼ teaspoon ground black pepper

Chopped fresh flat-leaf parsley

4 SERVINGS

Grilled Fresh Tuna Salad

INGREDIENTS

Dressing

3 tablespoon fresh lime juice

1 tablespoon white wine vinegar

1½ tablespoons extra virgin olive oil

1 tablespoon reduced-sodium
 soy sauce

Salt and ground black pepper

Nonstick cooking spray

4 4-ounce fresh tuna steaks, lightly
 seasoned with salt and pepper

4 large button mushrooms, cleaned
 and sliced

¼ cup sliced scallions

8 cups torn bibb lettuce

4 SERVINGS

Whisk all dressing ingredients in a small bowl. Season to taste with salt and pepper; set aside.

Spray grill grate with nonstick cooking spray, then preheat to medium-high. Grill steaks about 4 to 5 minutes per side, depending on thickness. Remove to a cutting board. Slice into strips and place in a large bowl. Add mushrooms, scallions and half the salad dressing; toss gently.

Toss lettuce in another bowl with remaining salad dressing. Line 4 dinner plates with lettuce. Place equal amounts of tuna mixture on top. Serve immediately. Refrigerate leftovers.

Grilled sourdough bread will complement this meal.

One serving contains approximately: Calories 235, Fat 11g, Carbohydrates 5g, Protein 29g

Grilled Salmon Caesar Salad

Mash garlic and anchovy paste with a fork on a clean cutting board; scrape into a bowl. Whisk in lemon juice, pepper sauce, Worcestershire sauce, black pepper and olive oil until well blended. Pour mixture over salmon in a large bowl and let sit while grill preheats.

Cook fish on heated grill about 4 minutes per side or until it reaches an internal temperature of 150°F and flakes easily when tested with a fork.

Mix lettuce, salad dressing and croutons in a bowl; divide mixture equally among 4 large salad or regular dinner plates. Top each with warm fish. Serve immediately. Refrigerate leftovers.

Add a few ripe grape tomatoes to salad for extra color, if desired.

One serving contains approximately: Calories 400, Fat 33g, Carbohydrates 8g, Protein 19g

INGREDIENTS

3 cloves fresh garlic, minced

1 tablespoon anchovy paste

¼ cup fresh lemon juice

¼ teaspoon Tabasco sauce

1 tablespoon Worcestershire sauce

½ teaspoon ground black pepper

⅓ cup olive oil

12-ounce salmon fillet, cut into 4 pieces

1 10-ounce bag torn romaine lettuce, washed

½ cup Caesar salad dressing

Croutons

4 SERVINGS

Grilled Salmon over Baby Greens

INGREDIENTS

4 6-ounce fresh salmon fillets

½ cup extra virgin olive oil

¼ cup balsamic vinegar

1 tablespoon honey

½ teaspoon salt

¼ teaspoon ground black pepper

6 cups baby greens or spring mix
   salad mixture

1 ripe tomato cut into wedges

4 SERVINGS

Rinse salmon and pat dry with paper towels.

Mix olive oil, vinegar, honey, salt, and pepper in a small container until well blended. Spoon 1 tablespoon mixture all over fish. Place fish on an oiled grill about 4 to 5 inches above medium coals. Cook, turning once, about 8 to 10 minutes, or until fish reaches an internal temperature of 150°F and flakes easily.

Line 4 plates with equal amounts of salad greens. Place warm fish over each and drizzle with remaining vinegar mixture. Garnish with tomatoes. Serve immediately. Refrigerate leftovers.

Grilling is one quick way to enjoy salmon.

One serving contains approximately: Calories 585, Fat 45g, Carbohydrates 9g, Protein 36g

Grilled Salmon Panzanella

Grill salmon on a preheated (high) oiled grill, about 5 minutes on each side or until cooked through. Remove from grill; set aside.

Mix vinegar, olives, capers and pepper in a large bowl. Whisk in olive oil. Fold in toasted bread, tomatoes, zucchini, cucumber, onion and basil.

Line 4 plates with lettuce. Place equal portions of bread salad mixture on lettuce. Top each with salmon. Serve immediately. Refrigerate leftovers.

Serve this delicious bread salad for a special meal.

Variation: Use toasted baguette pieces instead of whole grain bread.

One serving contains approximately: Calories 370, Fat 21g, Carbohydrates 15g, Protein 29g

INGREDIENTS

1 pound skinless salmon cut into 4 equal portions, lightly seasoned with salt and freshly ground black pepper

3 tablespoons red wine vinegar

8 kalamata olives, pitted and chopped

1 tablespoon capers, rinsed and chopped, or 1 sour pickle, chopped

¼ teaspoon ground back pepper

3 tablespoons extra virgin olive oil

2 slices whole grain bread, cubed and toasted in oven

2 fresh tomatoes, cut into bite-size pieces

1 small fresh zucchini, cubed

1 fresh cucumber, seeded and cubed

Half of a small red onion, thinly sliced

¼ cup torn fresh basil

Shredded iceberg lettuce

4 SERVINGS

Grilled Scallops Salad

INGREDIENTS

Salsa

2 red grapefruit, peeled, cut into halved segments, membranes removed

2 medium-size seedless oranges, peeled and cut into halved segments

1 tablespoon fresh lime juice

¼ cup chopped red onion

2 tablespoons chopped fresh cilantro leaves

1 pound sea scallops

1 tablespoon extra virgin olive oil

½ teaspoon salt

Mixed salad greens

4 SERVINGS

Toss grapefruit, orange segments, lime juice, onion and cilantro in a medium-size bowl; set aside.

Heat an indoor grill pan to medium-high. Toss scallops and olive oil in a bowl. Sprinkle with salt. Grill turning once, until opaque, about 4 to 6 minutes. Serve immediately over mixed salad greens along with fruit salsa. Refrigerate leftovers

Serve this light meal with warm rolls.

One serving contains approximately: Calories 280, Fat 5g, Carbohydrates 28g, Protein 33g

Grilled Shrimp and Cannellini Bean Salad

Mix fresh shrimp with 1 tablespoon olive oil, salt and black pepper in a medium bowl; set aside.

Heat 1 tablespoon olive oil in a medium nonstick saucepan. Add garlic; stir and cook 1 minute. Reduce heat to low. Add beans; cover and cook until warm, about 3 minutes.

Heat indoor grill pan. Add coated shrimp; grill about 3 minutes or until lightly browned and thoroughly cooked. Place in a large bowl. Add warm beans, lemon zest, lemon juice and tomatoes. Season with salt to taste.

Line 4 salad plates with fresh arugula. Top each equally with shrimp mixture. Serve immediately. Refrigerate leftovers.

Arugula has a slight peppery flavor. Use other salad greens if preferred.

One serving contains approximately: Calories 300, Fat 9g, Carbohydrates 30g, Protein 23g

INGREDIENTS

1 pound fresh shrimp, shelled and deveined, tails removed

2 tablespoons olive oil, divided

¼ teaspoon salt, or to taste

¼ teaspoon ground black pepper

2 cloves garlic, chopped

3 cups canned cannellini beans or navy beans, rinsed and drained

½ teaspoon fresh lemon zest

1 tablespoon fresh lemon juice

1 cup cherry tomatoes, halved

Fresh arugula

4 SERVINGS

Halibut Avocado Chickpea Salad

INGREDIENTS

4 4-ounce pieces halibut

½ teaspoon salt

¼ teaspoon ground black pepper

¼ cup extra virgin olive oil

1 tablespoon fresh lemon juice

1 tablespoon Dijon mustard

2 tablespoons chopped fresh cilantro

½ teaspoon salt

⅛ teaspoon ground black pepper

8 cups mixed salad greens

1 15-ounce can chickpeas, drained

1 avocado, peeled, pitted and sliced

Half of a small red onion, thinly sliced

4 SERVINGS

Season fish with salt and pepper. Place fish in a large skillet. Add enough water to reach halfway up the sides of fish. Bring to a simmer over medium heat. Cover and cook until fish is opaque throughout, about 6 to 8 minutes. Remove from skillet to a plate; cool. Flake fish with a fork into large pieces.

Whisk olive oil, lemon juice, mustard, cilantro, salt and pepper in a large bowl.

Add salad greens, chickpeas, avocado and red onion to bowl; toss. Place equal amounts of salad mixture on 4 plates. Top each equally with fish.

Garnish with lemon wedges. Serve with warm bread.

One serving contains approximately: Calories 411, Fat 24g, Carbohydrates 20g, Protein 31g

Lobster Asparagus Salad

Whisk all dressing ingredients in a small container until blended.

Cut lobster tails, using a kitchen shears, lengthwise through centers of top shells and meat, cutting to, but not through, bottom of shells. Spread halves of tail apart.

Place a steamer basket in a saucepan. Add water to just below bottom of basket. Bring water to a boil. Add lobster. Reduce heat; cover and steam 8 minutes. Add asparagus; cover and continue steaming 3 minutes or until lobster is opaque. Remove lobster and asparagus from basket. When cool enough to handle, remove meat from shells and coarsely chop. Cut asparagus into 1½-inch pieces.

Line a serving platter with lettuce. Place lobster and asparagus on lettuce. Drizzle with dressing; sprinkle with bacon and cheese. Garnish with red grape tomatoes. Serve. Refrigerate leftovers.

Make this salad for a special supper. Serve with butter crackers.

One serving contains approximately: Calories 250, Fat 12g, Carbohydrates 8g, Protein 28g

INGREDIENTS

Dressing

½ teaspoon shredded fresh lemon peel

2 tablespoons fresh lemon juice

2 tablespoons extra virgin olive oil

1 tablespoon minced shallots

2 teaspoons snipped fresh dill

2 teaspoons honey

¼ teaspoon salt

¼ teaspoon ground black pepper

2 8-ounce fresh lobster tails

1 pound fresh tender asparagus spears

4 cups torn butter, Boston or bibb lettuce

3 slices bacon, crisply cooked, drained and crumbled

¼ cup shaved Parmesan cheese

Red grape tomatoes

4 SERVINGS

Maine Lobster Salad

INGREDIENTS

¼ cup butter (not margarine), melted

1 pound cooked lobster meat, cut into bite-size pieces

¼ cup mayonnaise

Salt, to taste

⅛ teaspoon ground white pepper

¼ cup finely chopped celery

Butter lettuce

4 SERVINGS

Pour butter over lobster pieces in a medium bowl; toss until coated. Stir in mayonnaise, salt, pepper and celery. Cover and chill slightly before serving. Serve over a bed of butter lettuce. Refrigerate leftovers.

Serve with warm croissants.

Variation: Add cooked sweet peas.

One serving contains approximately: Calories 305, Fat 24g, Carbohydrates 4g, Protein 21g

Mary Dow's Tuna Salad

Cook macaroni following package directions. Drain in a colander and rinse with cold water, then drain well. Place in a large bowl.

Add celery, bell pepper, onion, eggs, tuna, salt, pepper and mayonnaise to bowl. Stir gently until combined. Serve at room temperature, or cover and chill slightly before serving. Serve over lettuce. Refrigerate leftovers.

Garnish each serving with sliced fresh tomatoes and pickles. Serve with warm, soft rolls . . . buttered, of course.

One serving contains approximately: Calories 589, Fat 34g, Carbohydrates 56g, Protein 32g

INGREDIENTS

1 12-ounce package uncooked elbow macaroni

¾ cup finely chopped celery

½ cup chopped green bell pepper

1 tablespoon finely chopped yellow onion

3 hard-boiled eggs, coarsely chopped

2 6-ounce cans tuna, drained

½ teaspoon salt, or to taste

¼ teaspoon ground black pepper

⅔ cup mayonnaise, or to taste

6 SERVINGS

Pan-Seared Scallops with Wilted Spinach Salad

INGREDIENTS

1 pound fresh sea scallops

2 tablespoons all-purpose flour

2 teaspoons blackened-steak
  seasoning

1 tablespoon cooking oil

10 ounces fresh spinach

1 tablespoon water

2 tablespoons balsamic vinegar

4 ounces bacon, diced and cooked
  crisp, crumbled

4 SERVINGS

Rinse scallops; pat dry. Put flour and seasoning in a plastic food storage bag. Add scallops; toss to coat. Heat oil in a large non-stick skillet over medium heat. Add scallops; cook, turning once until browned and opaque, about 6 minutes. Remove scallops.

Add spinach to same skillet; sprinkle with water. Cover and cook over medium-high heat until wilted, about 2 minutes. Add vinegar; toss to coat. Return scallops to skillet with spinach. Heat thoroughly. Sprinkle each serving with crumbled bacon and serve immediately. Refrigerate leftovers.

Serve with warm crusty bread.

One serving contains approximately: Calories 292, Fat 21g, Carbohydrates 11g, Protein 28g

Pasta Salad with Tuna and Fresh Herbs

Cook pasta according to package directions. Drain in a colander and rinse with cold water until cold then drain again.

Whisk olive oil, lemon juice, salt, garlic powder and lemon zest in a large bowl. Add pasta.

Add tomatoes, tuna, olives, onion, parsley, basil and oregano. Toss to combine. Serve immediately or cover and chill until ready to serve. Refrigerate leftovers.

Garnish with pickles and serve with breadsticks.

One serving contains approximately: Calories 561, Fat 26g, Carbohydrates 60g, Protein 23g

INGREDIENTS

1 pound uncooked fusilli pasta

½ cup extra virgin olive oil

¼ cup fresh lemon juice

½ teaspoon salt

¼ teaspoon garlic powder

½ teaspoon grated fresh lemon zest

2 cups halved cherry tomatoes

1 12-ounce can oil-packed tuna, drained and flaked

½ cup pitted black olives, chopped

Half of a small red onion, thinly sliced and pulled into rings

¼ cup chopped fresh flat-leaf parsley

2 tablespoons chopped fresh basil leaves

1 tablespoon chopped fresh oregano

6 SERVINGS

Quinoa Tuna Salad

INGREDIENTS

½ **cup uncooked quinoa**

1 **cup water**

¼ **cup chopped celery**

¼ **cup chopped yellow onion**

¼ **cup low-fat mayonnaise**

1 **teaspoon fresh lemon juice**

1 **teaspoon wasabi powder or jarred grated horseradish**

¼ **teaspoon salt, or to taste**

¼ **teaspoon ground black pepper**

1 **6-ounce can tuna, drained**

2 SERVINGS

Mix quinoa and water in a microwave-safe bowl. Cover and microwave on high until water is absorbed and quinoa is tender, about 9 minutes. Spoon into a medium-size bowl; chill slightly.

Add celery, onion, mayonnaise, lemon juice, wasabi powder, salt and black pepper to the bowl with the cooked quinoa. Mix well. Gently stir in tuna. Chill slightly. Serve. Refrigerate leftovers.

Garnish with sliced fresh tomatoes. Serve with warm breadsticks.

One serving contains approximately: Calories 318, Fat 6g, Carbohydrates 39g, Protein 27g

Ruth's Shrimp Salad

Line 4 salad bowls with lettuce. Sprinkle each with equal amounts of sliced celery. Top equally with sliced tomatoes. Divide shrimp equally and arrange over sliced tomatoes.

Whisk all dressing ingredients in a small bowl until well blended. Drizzle dressing over each salad. Serve immediately. Refrigerate leftovers.

My sister Ruth always has shrimp on the menu! Enjoy this quick meal with warm French bread.

One serving contains approximately: Calories 258, Fat 12g, Carbohydrates 14g, Protein 26g

INGREDIENTS

Shredded iceberg lettuce

4 ribs celery, thinly sliced

4 large, ripe fresh tomatoes, sliced

1 pound cooked Louisiana jumbo shrimp, tails removed

Dressing

5 tablespoons purchased prepared horseradish

2 teaspoons brown sugar

¼ teaspoon salt

⅛ teaspoon ground black pepper

⅓ cup fresh tomato juice

3 tablespoons extra virgin olive oil

1 tablespoon fresh lemon juice

1 teaspoon Tabasco sauce

4 SERVINGS

Salmon and Raspberry Salad

INGREDIENTS

4 fresh salmon fillets

¾ cup balsamic vinaigrette, divided

8 cups spring mix salad greens

1 cup fresh raspberries, rinsed and patted dry

½ cup toasted chopped walnuts

4 SERVINGS

Rinse fish and pat dry. Brush fillets with ¼ cup vinaigrette. Place on a grill over medium heat and cook about 5 minutes per side or until fish reaches an internal temperature of 150°F and flakes easily when tested with a fork. Remove from grill; keep warm.

Line 4 dinner plates equally with salad greens. Top each with equal amounts of raspberries and walnuts. Place cooked salmon over salad and drizzle each with remaining vinaigrette. Serve. Refrigerate leftovers.

Toasted French bread will complement this warm salad supper.

One serving contains approximately: Calories 360, Fat 16g, Carbohydrates 29g, Protein 26g

Salmon Pesto Pasta Salad

Cook pasta according to package directions. Drain in a colander. Place in a large bowl and cool slightly; toss with garlic, pesto and salad dressing.

Microwave zucchini, covered, in a microwave-safe dish on high for 2 minutes; add to pasta mixture. Add tomatoes, onion and peas; toss. Gently fold in salmon. Season with salt and pepper. Serve immediately.

Serve this delicious salad with warm rolls.

One serving contains approximately: Calories 310, Fat 16g, Carbohydrates 26g, Protein 17g

INGREDIENTS

8 ounces uncooked small shell pasta

3 cloves fresh garlic, minced

½ cup prepared basil pesto

½ cup light Italian salad dressing

1 fresh zucchini, cut in round ½-inch slices, then cut in half

1 pint cherry tomatoes, halved

1 small red onion, thinly sliced

1 cup frozen petite peas, thawed

2 7.5-ounce cans salmon, drained and broken into bite-size pieces

¼ teaspoon salt, or to taste

¼ teaspoon ground black pepper

8 SERVINGS

Salmon Rice Salad

INGREDIENTS

1 tablespoon extra virgin olive oil

6 green onions, bottoms thinly sliced (reserve green tops)

1 pound skinless fresh salmon fillets, cut into 1-inch pieces, seasoned with ¼ teaspoon black pepper

3 cups cooked white rice

¼ cup teriyaki sauce

Reserved green onion tops, chopped

1 tablespoon chopped flat-leaf parsley leaves

4 SERVINGS

Heat olive oil in a large nonstick skillet over medium heat until hot. Add sliced onions; cook and stir 2 minutes. Add salmon to skillet with onions; cook and stir until opaque in centers, about 7 minutes.

Remove skillet from heat. Stir in rice and teriyaki sauce. Place equal amounts of mixture into 4 salad bowls. Sprinkle with chopped green onion tops and parsley leaves. Serve immediately. Refrigerate leftovers.

Garnish each serving with grape tomatoes. Serve with French bread.

One serving contains approximately: Calories 410, Fat 9g, Carbohydrates 48g, Protein 28g

Salmon Spinach Cabbage Salad

Put all dressing ingredients in a blender; process until smooth.

Put salad greens, spinach, red cabbage, snow peas and chives in a large bowl; toss. Drizzle with salad dressing; toss to coat.

Place equal amounts of salad mixture on 4 individual plates. Top each equally with crumbled salmon. Serve immediately. Refrigerate leftovers.

Serve with warm whole wheat rolls.

Variation: Use canned salmon, drained and flaked, and Italian vinaigrette dressing.

One serving contains approximately: Calories 128, Fat 2g, Carbohydrates 17g, Protein 11g

INGREDIENTS

Dressing

¼ **cup all-fruit apricot spread**

¼ **cup fresh orange juice**

2 **tablespoons white wine vinegar**

2 **teaspoons granulated sugar**

¼ **teaspoon ground ginger**

⅛ **teaspoon crushed red pepper flakes**

⅛ **teaspoon salt**

Salad

4 **cups spring mix salad greens, torn into bite-size pieces**

2 **cups fresh baby spinach leaves**

1 **cup shredded red cabbage**

1 **cup snow peas, trimmed and cut in half diagonally**

1 **tablespoon chopped fresh chives**

1 **7.1-ounce vacuum-sealed pouch pink salmon, crumbled**

4 SERVINGS

Salmon Summer Salad

INGREDIENTS

1 small head iceberg lettuce,
   torn into pieces

Half a head of romaine lettuce,
   torn into pieces

1 8-ounce container sliced
   white mushrooms

2 ripe medium-size tomatoes,
   cut into wedges

1 medium-size green bell pepper,
   cut into rings

2 7.1-ounce packages skinless and
   boneless pink salmon

¾ cup Italian salad dressing

6 SERVINGS

Mix lettuce, mushrooms, tomatoes and bell pepper in a large salad bowl. Flake in salmon. Add salad dressing and toss just before serving. Refrigerate leftovers.

Substitute canned salmon, if desired, drained, with skin and bones discarded.

One serving contains approximately: Calories 210, Fat 11g, Carbohydrates 11g, Protein 18g

Salmon Vegetable Pasta Salad

Cook pasta according to package directions. Place cooked pasta in a large bowl.

Mix chickpeas, tomatoes, zucchini, olives and salmon in a large nonstick skillet; bring to a boil, stirring constantly. Reduce heat; simmer uncovered 5 minutes. Spoon mixture over hot pasta. Top with cheese. Serve immediately. Refrigerate leftovers.

Serve this hearty salad along with crisp whole wheat breadsticks.

One serving contains approximately: Calories 680, Fat 4g, Carbohydrates 118g, Protein 35g

INGREDIENTS

1 16-ounce package uncooked penne pasta

1 15-ounce can chickpeas, drained

1 14.5-ounce can diced tomatoes with basil, garlic and oregano

1 medium-size fresh zucchini, sliced ¼-inch thick

2 tablespoons sliced ripe olives

1 6-ounce pouch premium skinless, boneless pink salmon

½ cup grated Parmesan cheese

4 SERVINGS

Salmon with Olive Oil and Herbs

INGREDIENTS

2 tablespoons extra virgin olive oil

18 ounces fresh salmon fillets

½ cup extra virgin olive oil

¼ cup fresh lemon juice

¼ cup fresh lime juice

2 tablespoons chopped fresh parsley

2 tablespoons chopped fresh cilantro

2 tablespoons chopped fresh dill

¼ teaspoon salt

¼ teaspoon ground black pepper

6 cups mixed salad greens

6 SERVINGS

Preheat oven to 350°F. Heat and brush a grill pan with 2 table-spoons olive oil. Grill fillets, for 4 minutes on each side, starting with the skin side up.

Mix ½ cup olive oil, lemon juice, lime juice, parsley, cilantro, dill, salt and pepper in a small bowl; set aside.

Remove fillets from pan and place in a large shallow baking pan. Brush with olive oil-herb mixture. Bake in preheated oven, about 3 to 4 minutes or until fillets flake easily with a fork. Remove from oven. Serve immediately over salad greens. Refrigerate leftovers.

Garnish with tomato and lemon wedges. Serve with warm rolls.

One serving contains approximately: Calories 365, Fat 37g, Carbohydrates 7g, Protein 24g

Sesame Shrimp Pasta Salad

Mix all dressing ingredients in bowl until well blended; set aside.

Cook pasta according to package directions. Add asparagus during last minute of cooking time. Drain in a colander; rinse with cold water until cool. Place in a large bowl.

Add shrimp, bell pepper, green onions and ¼ cup cilantro to pasta mixture. Add dressing; toss to combine. Sprinkle with ¼ cup cilantro and sesame seeds. Serve. Refrigerate leftovers.

Toasted sesame seeds enhance this good salad.

One serving contains approximately: Calories 500, Fat 12g, Carbohydrates 67g, Protein 30g

INGREDIENTS

Dressing

¼ cup peanut butter

¼ cup rice wine vinegar

¼ cup light soy sauce

2 tablespoons sesame oil

2 tablespoons brown sugar

2 garlic cloves, pressed

1 tablespoon minced fresh ginger

½ teaspoon red pepper flakes

¼ cup hot water

1 pound uncooked penne rigati pasta

½ pound fresh asparagus, cut into ½-inch slices

1 pound cooked medium-size shrimp, tails removed

1 fresh red bell pepper cut into thin strips

4 green onions, thinly sliced

½ cup chopped fresh cilantro or flat-leaf parsley, divided

Toasted sesame seeds

4–6 SERVINGS

Shells and Tuna Salad

INGREDIENTS

4 cups uncooked pasta shells

1½ cups frozen sweet peas, thawed

2 ribs celery, coarsely chopped

½ cup chopped red onion

½ cup chopped green bell pepper

½ cup chopped fresh flat-leaf parsley

2 6-ounce cans tuna, drained

⅓ cup extra virgin olive oil

¼ cup red wine vinegar

½ teaspoon Dijon mustard

1 teaspoon salt

¼ teaspoon ground black pepper

4 SERVINGS

Cook pasta according to package directions. Drain and rinse with cold water, then drain again; place in a large bowl. Add peas, celery, onion, bell pepper, parsley and tuna to the bowl.

Whisk olive oil, vinegar, mustard, salt and black pepper in a small container. Pour over pasta mixture; toss to combine. Serve immediately. Refrigerate leftovers.

Garnish each serving with sliced fresh tomatoes and serve with warm rolls.

One serving contains approximately: Calories 585, Fat 20g, Carbohydrates 65g, Protein 35g

Shrimp and Avocado Salad

Bring water, wine, 1 teaspoon salt and bay leaf to a boil in a medium saucepan. Reduce heat; simmer 5 minutes. Add half the shrimp, cook until opaque, about 3 minutes; remove from saucepan. Cook remaining shrimp as before; remove from saucepan. Cut shrimp into ¼-inch pieces.

Whisk lemon juice, vinegar and 1 teaspoon salt in a medium-size glass bowl. Whisk in olive oil until emulsified. Whisk in crème fraîche. Fold in chives, shallot and shrimp. Chill. Fold endives and avocado into shrimp mixture. Serve over a bed of butter lettuce. Refrigerate leftovers

Make this tasty salad for a special supper.

One serving contains approximately: Calories 480, Fat 30g, Carbohydrates 17g, Protein 29g

INGREDIENTS

2 cups water

1 cup dry white wine

2 teaspoons coarse salt, divided

1 dried bay leaf

1 pound medium-size fresh shrimp, peeled, divided

2 tablespoons fresh lemon juice

1 tablespoon white wine vinegar

¼ cup extra virgin olive oil

6 tablespoons crème fraîche

2 tablespoons minced fresh chives

2 tablespoons finely chopped shallot

2 small Belgian endives, leaves separated and thinly sliced crosswise

1 ripe, fresh California avocado, peeled, pitted and diced

1 small head butter lettuce

4 SERVINGS

Shrimp and Feta Salad

INGREDIENTS

¼ cup bottled lemon and chive salad dressing, divided

1 pound large shrimp, shelled and deveined

1 6-ounce bag mixed baby greens

2 tablespoons snipped fresh chives

2 ounces crumbled feta cheese

4 SERVINGS

Heat 1 tablespoon salad dressing in a large nonstick skillet. Add shrimp; stir and cook until shrimp are thoroughly cooked, about 8 minutes.

Place salad greens in a large bowl; toss with remaining 3 tablespoons salad dressing. Place equal amounts on 4 large salad plates. Top equally with shrimp, chives and cheese. Serve immediately. Refrigerate leftovers.

Garnish each serving with ½ cup diced seedless watermelon. Serve with toasted French baguette slices.

One serving contains approximately: Calories 280, Fat 14g, Carbohydrates 10g, Protein 27g

Shrimp and Macaroni Salad

Cook pasta according to package directions; drain in a colander and rinse with cold water, then drain again. Place in a large bowl.

Add shrimp, celery, onion and bell pepper to bowl with pasta; mix well.

Whisk all dressing ingredients in a small container until blender. Add to pasta mixture in bowl; mix well. Cover and chill slightly before serving. Refrigerate leftovers.

Garnish with red grape tomatoes. Serve with warm crusty rolls.

One serving contains approximately: Calories 778, Fat 50g, Carbohydrates 60g, Protein 24g

INGREDIENTS

1 16-ounce package uncooked elbow macaroni

1½ pounds cooked medium-size shrimp, tails removed, cut in half crosswise

1 cup finely chopped celery

½ cup finely chopped yellow onion

¼ cup finely chopped green bell pepper

Dressing

1½ cups mayonnaise

¾ cup French salad dressing

1 tablespoon granulated sugar

1 tablespoon white vinegar

1 teaspoon salt

1 teaspoon black pepper

1 teaspoon garlic powder

1 teaspoon paprika

8 SERVINGS

Shrimp Caesar Salad

INGREDIENTS

1½ **pounds fresh raw shrimp, peeled and deveined, tails removed**

1 **cup fat-free seasoned croutons**

2 **tablespoons grated Parmesan cheese**

1 **10-ounce package chopped romaine lettuce**

Dressing

2 **tablespoons light mayonnaise**

2 **tablespoons cold water**

2 **tablespoons fresh lemon juice**

1 **teaspoon grated Parmesan cheese**

¼ **teaspoon ground black pepper**

¼ **teaspoon hot pepper sauce**

⅛ **teaspoon Worcestershire sauce**

2 **cloves garlic, minced**

3 **tablespoons toasted chopped nuts**

Chopped fresh flat-leaf parsley

4 SERVINGS

In a medium-size pot, cook the raw shrimp in boiling water about 3 minutes or until done; drain. Place in a large bowl and chill slightly.

Add croutons, cheese and romaine lettuce to bowl.

Whisk all salad dressing ingredients in a small bowl; add to salad. Toss to coat. Top with nuts and parsley. Serve immediately. Refrigerate leftovers.

Precooked shrimp may be used instead of raw shrimp, if desired.

One serving contains approximately: Calories 295, Fat 10g, Carbohydrates 12g, Protein 39g

Shrimp Couscous Salad

Pour 1 cup boiling water over couscous in a large bowl. Cover and let stand 5 minutes, then fluff with a fork.

Mix remaining ingredients in a large bowl. Serve immediately over the cooked couscous. Refrigerate leftovers.

Serve topped with Parmesan cheese, if desired.

One serving contains approximately: Calories 453, Fat 2g, Carbohydrates 46g, Protein 43g

INGREDIENTS

1 cup uncooked couscous, mixed with ¼ teaspoon salt and ¼ teaspoon ground black pepper

1½ pounds cooked, peeled and deveined medium-size shrimp, tails removed

½ pound snap peas, cut into small pieces (ends snipped and discarded)

2 cups cherry tomatoes, halved

½ cup torn fresh basil leaves

2 green onions, thinly sliced

2 tablespoons extra virgin olive oil

2 teaspoons finely grated lemon zest

3 tablespoons fresh lemon juice

¾ teaspoon salt

¼ teaspoon ground black pepper

4 SERVINGS

Shrimp Salad with Fresh Orange

INGREDIENTS

1 pound cooked, peeled and deveined shrimp, tails removed

1 small head Boston lettuce, torn

1 small head romaine lettuce, torn

1 cup watercress

1 cup finely chopped celery

1 small yellow onion, sliced into thin rings

15 pitted ripe olives, sliced

½ cup Italian salad dressing

12 cherry tomatoes

2 small oranges, peeled and sectioned

6 SERVINGS

Place all ingredients except oranges in a large bowl. Toss until coated.

Place equal amounts of salad on 6 plates. Garnish each with orange sections. Drizzle lightly with more Italian salad dressing, if desired. Serve. Refrigerate leftovers.

This is a good salad for those warm summer nights.

One serving contains approximately: Calories 210, Fat 9g, Carbohydrates 14g, Protein 17g

Shrimp Salad with Tortilla

Preheat oven to 400°F. Toss tortilla strips with 1 tablespoon olive oil and ¼ teaspoon salt on a baking sheet; arrange in a single layer. Bake until crisp, about 7 minutes; place in a bowl.

Mix all dressing ingredients and 3 tablespoons olive oil in a small container until well blended; set aside.

Heat 1 tablespoon olive oil in large nonstick skillet over medium-high heat. Add shrimp; cook about 3 minutes per side or until done. Place in a large bowl. Add romaine hearts, cabbage and avocado. Pour dressing mixture over all; toss gently until coated. Serve immediately topped with tortillas and roasted seeds. Refrigerate leftovers

Use purchased oil and vinegar dressing, if preferred.

One serving contains approximately: Calories 588, Fat 5g, Carbohydrates 31g, Protein 44g

INGREDIENTS

6 corn tortillas, cut into strips

5 tablespoons extra virgin olive oil, divided

¼ teaspoon salt

Dressing

2 tablespoons fresh orange juice

2 tablespoons fresh lime juice

½ teaspoon salt

¼ teaspoon ground black pepper

1½ pounds peeled and deveined fresh raw large shrimp, seasoned with ½ teaspoon ground cumin, ¼ teaspoon salt and ¼ teaspoon black pepper

5 cups thinly sliced romaine hearts

3 cups thinly sliced green cabbage

1 ripe avocado, peeled pitted and sliced

¼ cup roasted pumpkin seeds

4 SERVINGS

Smoked Salmon Pasta Salad

INGREDIENTS

2 cups uncooked bow tie pasta

Dressing

¼ cup red wine vinegar

2 tablespoons chopped fresh basil

1 tablespoon cold water

1 teaspoon granulated sugar

⅛ teaspoon ground black pepper

3 cups fresh spinach leaves, cleaned, stems discarded

1 cup halved cherry tomatoes

½ cup thinly sliced cucumber

¼ pound reduced-fat Swiss cheese, cut into bite-size cubes

4 ounces smoked salmon, cut into bite-size pieces

4 SERVINGS

Cook pasta according to package directions. Rinse with cold water and drain.

Whisk all dressing ingredients in a small container until well blended.

Mix all ingredients except salad dressing in a large bowl. Pour salad dressing over all and toss gently to coat. Serve. Refrigerate leftovers.

Use leftover cooked salmon instead of smoked salmon . . . about 1 cup.

One serving contains approximately: Calories 230, Fat 5g, Carbohydrates 30g, Protein 15g

Soba Noodles Salmon Salad

Cook noodles according to package directions. Drain. Rinse with cold water until cold. Drain again. Place in a large bowl.

Rinse fish and pat dry with paper towels. Season with salt and pepper. Heat oil in a large nonstick skillet over medium heat until hot. Add fish. Cook until opaque throughout, turning once, about 5 to 6 minutes per side. Place on a cutting board and break into pieces.

Add bell pepper, green onions, mint and vinaigrette to bowl with pasta; toss until coated. Place equal amounts of mixture into 4 salad bowls. Top each equally with salmon. Serve. Refrigerate leftovers.

Serve with crisp rice crackers.

One serving contains approximately: Calories 568, Fat 22g, Carbohydrates 43g, Protein 47g

INGREDIENTS

8 ounces uncooked soba noodles

4 6-ounce fresh skinless salmon fillets

½ teaspoon salt

¼ teaspoon ground black pepper

1 tablespoon vegetable oil

1 red bell pepper, seeded and sliced

4 green onions, thinly sliced

1 teaspoon minced fresh mint

¼ cup ginger vinaigrette

4 SERVINGS

Tangy Avocado Shrimp Salad

INGREDIENTS

6 cups torn romaine lettuce

½ cup extra virgin olive oil

⅓ cup fresh lime juice

⅓ cup minced yellow onion

3 tablespoons minced fresh cilantro,
   or flat-leaf parsley

3 tablespoons white vinegar

2 tablespoons finely chopped seeded
   jalapeño pepper, or to taste

1½ teaspoons minced fresh garlic

1 teaspoon salt

¼ teaspoon ground black pepper

½ pound cooked small shrimp

1 ripe avocado, peeled, pitted
   and sliced

1 ripe tomato and cut into wedges

4 SERVINGS

Place lettuce in a large bowl. Whisk olive oil, lime juice, onion, cilantro, vinegar, jalapeño, garlic, salt and black pepper in a small container until blended; add to lettuce; toss to coat.

Line 4 plates equally with lettuce. Top each equally with shrimp and avocado. Garnish with tomato. Serve. Refrigerate leftovers.

Serve with crusty rolls.

One serving contains approximately: Calories 397, Fat 35g, Carbohydrates 9g, Protein 15g

Thai Seafood Salad

Mix lime juice, fish sauce, sugar and chili paste in a small bowl.

In a large skillet, bring water to a simmer over medium heat. Add scallops; cover and cook 3 minutes or until done. Remove from skillet; place in a large bowl. Add shrimp to simmering water in same skillet; cover and cook about 3 minutes or until done. Remove from skillet; add to scallops.

Add lime juice mixture, bell pepper, onion, mint, crabmeat, lemongrass and cucumber to bowl; toss to combine. Refrigerate leftovers.

Lemongrass is commonly used in Thai cooking. You can substitute fresh lemon juice if lemongrass is not readily available.

One serving contains approximately: Calories 180, Fat 3g, Carbohydrates 9g, Protein 30g

INGREDIENTS

5 tablespoons fresh lime juice

2½ tablespoons fish sauce

1 teaspoon granulated sugar

1 teaspoon chili paste with garlic

½ cup water

8 ounces sea scallops

1 pound peeled and deveined fresh medium-size shrimp, tails removed

1 cup fresh red bell pepper strips

½ cup chopped red onion

¼ cup fresh mint leaves, finely chopped

8 ounces lump crabmeat, drained and shell pieces removed

2 fresh lemongrass stalks, trimmed and thinly sliced

1 cucumber, thinly sliced into half-moon shapes

6 SERVINGS

Thai Shrimp Noodle Salad

INGREDIENTS

8 ounces uncooked fettuccine pasta

2 cups 1-inch pieces of tender
   fresh asparagus

2 cups cooked shrimp

1 medium red bell pepper cut into
   matchstick strips

½ cup thinly sliced scallions

1 8-ounce can bamboo shoots,
   drained

Dressing

¼ cup chicken broth

¼ cup seasoned rice vinegar

2 tablespoons reduced-sodium
   soy sauce

2 tablespoons creamy peanut butter

1 tablespoon honey

2 large cloves garlic, crushed

1½ teaspoons grated ginger root
   or ½ teaspoon ground ginger

5 SERVINGS

Cook pasta according to package directions, adding asparagus 2 minutes before cooking time is up; drain in a colander and rinse with cold water, then drain again. Place in a large bowl.

Add shrimp, bell pepper, scallion and bamboo shoots to pasta in bowl.

Process all dressing ingredients in a blender until smooth. Pour dressing over pasta mixture; mix well. Cover and chill. Serve. Refrigerate leftovers.

Serve this tasty meal with warm crusty bread.

One serving contains approximately: Calories 682, Fat 12g, Carbohydrates 69g, Protein 78g

Tilapia Salad

Heat ¼ cup olive oil in a large nonstick skillet over medium-high heat until hot. Season fish with salt and black pepper; place in hot skillet and cook in batches until done, about 3 minutes per side. Place on a plate; cool and break into pieces.

Whisk ¼ cup olive oil, lime juice, mustard and honey in a small bowl; pour into a medium-size bowl. Add arugula, endive, apple and almonds; toss lightly. Serve on 4 individual salad plates topped equally with fish. Serve. Refrigerate leftovers.

Enjoy this fish salad with buttered corn sticks.

One serving contains approximately: Calories 424, Fat 24g, Carbohydrates 18g, Protein 39g

INGREDIENTS

½ cup extra virgin olive oil, divided

4 6-ounce tilapia fillets

½ teaspoon salt

¼ teaspoon freshly ground black pepper

2 tablespoons fresh lime juice

1 tablespoon Dijon mustard

2 teaspoons honey

6 cups arugula

2 heads endive, sliced

1 apple, thinly sliced

¼ cup toasted sliced almonds

4 SERVINGS

Tomatoes and Crab Salad

INGREDIENTS

¾ **cup sour cream**

2 **tablespoons chopped fresh dill**

1 **tablespoon Dijon mustard**

2½ **pounds ripe heirloom tomatoes, cored and chopped**

1 **pound cooked crabmeat**

¼ **cup chopped chives**

1 **teaspoon fresh lemon zest**

¼ **tablespoon fresh lemon juice**

¼ **teaspoon salt, or to taste**

⅛ **teaspoon ground white pepper**

Mixed salad greens

6 SERVINGS

Mix sour cream, dill and mustard in a small container; set aside.

Place tomatoes, crabmeat, chives, lemon zest, lemon juice, salt and pepper in a large bowl; toss gently to combine.

Line 6 plates with mixed salad greens. Spoon equal amounts crab salad mixture over greens. Serve with dollops of sour cream mixture on the side. Serve immediately. Refrigerate leftovers.

Colorful heirloom tomatoes are used in this salad; use other tomatoes if heirlooms are not readily available. Serve with warm croissants.

One serving contains approximately: Calories 140, Fat 4g, Carbohydrates 14g, Protein 19g

Tuna and Bean Bread Salad

Preheat broiler. Place baguette pieces on a rimmed baking sheet. Broil about 3 minutes or until bread is slightly browned. Remove from oven; set aside.

Mix beans, pickles, onion, olive oil, vinegar, salt and black pepper in a large bowl until well combined. Fold in toasted baguette pieces. Divide mixture equally on 4 plates or bowls. Top each equally with tuna, tomatoes and parsley. Serve immediately. Refrigerate leftovers.

Try a bruschetta salad . . . you will love it!

Variation: Use toasted cubed Italian bread instead of baguette pieces.

One serving contains approximately: Calories 398, Fat 17g, Carbohydrates 30g, Protein 27g

INGREDIENTS

Half of a baguette, torn into 2-inch pieces (about 4 cups) and mixed thoroughly with 1 tablespoon extra virgin olive oil

1 19-ounce can cannellini beans or chickpeas, rinsed and drained well

2 medium-size dill pickles cut into bite-size pieces

1 small red onion, very thinly sliced

3 tablespoons extra virgin olive oil

2 tablespoons red wine vinegar

½ teaspoon salt

¼ teaspoon freshly ground black pepper

2 6-ounce cans tuna, drained and flaked

1 cup grape tomatoes

2 tablespoons torn flat-leaf parsley

4 SERVINGS

Tuna and Bow Tie Salad

INGREDIENTS

8 ounces uncooked bow tie pasta

6 tablespoons light mayonnaise

2 tablespoons red wine vinegar

2 tablespoons chopped fresh basil, or 1 teaspoon dried basil leaves, crushed

1 clove fresh garlic, finely chopped

¼ teaspoon ground black pepper

2 6-ounce cans tuna, drained and flaked

1 9-ounce package frozen green beans, thawed, optional

2 cups cherry tomatoes, quartered

⅓ cup chopped red onion

4 SERVINGS

Cook pasta according to package directions; drain and rinse with cold water until cool. Place in a large bowl.

Mix mayonnaise, vinegar, basil, garlic and black pepper in a small container; add to pasta in bowl.

Add remaining ingredients to bowl. Mix well. Serve immediately or chill if desired. Refrigerate leftovers.

Variation: Substitute cooked peas for the green beans, if desired.

One serving contains approximately: Calories 410, Fat 9g, Carbohydrates 53g, Protein 33g

Tuna Rice Salad

Whisk olive oil, vinegar, salt and pepper in a large bowl until blended. Add rice; toss to coat. Add remaining ingredients; gently stir to combine.

Line 4 salad bowls with lettuce. Top each equally with rice-tuna mixture. Serve immediately. Refrigerate leftovers.

Garnish this tasty salad with sliced hard-boiled eggs and olives. Cooked rice can be found in the freezer section of food market.

One serving contains approximately: Calories 260, Fat 11g, Carbohydrates 26g, Protein 12g

INGREDIENTS

¼ **cup extra virgin olive oil**

¼ **cup cider vinegar**

¼ **teaspoon salt**

¼ **teaspoon ground black pepper**

3 cups cold cooked rice, white or brown

1 6-ounce can tuna, drained

2 ripe tomatoes, chopped

1 cup diced fresh cucumber

½ **cup sliced celery**

2 tablespoons chopped red onion

2 tablespoons chopped flat-leaf parsley

Shredded iceberg lettuce

4 SERVINGS

Tuna Spinach Salad

INGREDIENTS

1 7-ounce pouch albacore tuna

1 bunch fresh spinach, washed, stems discarded, coarsely torn

½ pound button mushrooms, cleaned and thinly sliced

Half of a medium-size red onion, thinly sliced

1 ripe avocado, peeled, pitted and cut into ½-inch cubes

½ cup Italian vinaigrette salad dressing, or to taste

¼ cup crumbled crisp cooked bacon

1 hard-boiled egg, finely chopped

6 SERVINGS

Place all ingredients except bacon and egg in a large bowl; toss. Sprinkle with bacon and egg. Serve. Refrigerate leftovers.

Garnish with pickle spears when serving. Serve with warm hard rolls.

One serving contains approximately: Calories 158, Fat 11g, Carbohydrates 7g, Protein 11g

Warm Cioppino Salad

Mix dressing ingredients in a small container; set aside.

Heat 1 tablespoon olive oil in a 10-inch nonstick skillet over medium heat until hot. Add shrimp; stir and cook until opaque in center, about 3 minutes; remove from skillet and place in a small bowl.

Heat 2 tablespoons olive oil in same skillet. Add mushrooms and zucchini; stir and cook until tender crisp, about 3 minutes. Return cooked shrimp to skillet along with tomatoes, olives and dressing mixture; stir gently until heated through.

To serve, place spinach in a large bowl; pour hot skillet mixture over greens; top with crab. Salt to taste; mix gently and serve immediately. Refrigerate leftovers.

Serve this seafood salad with warm chunks of sourdough bread.

One serving contains approximately: Calories 285, Fat 17g, Carbohydrates 17g, Protein 19g

INGREDIENTS

Dressing

¼ cup fresh lemon juice

1 tablespoon Worcestershire sauce

½ teaspoon dried basil

½ teaspoon dried oregano

2 cloves garlic, minced

3 tablespoons extra virgin olive oil, divided

½ pound fresh shrimp, peeled and deveined, tails removed

½ pound sliced fresh mushrooms

½ pound fresh zucchini, cut into ¼-inch thick slices

1 14.5-ounce can diced tomatoes, juice reserved

1½ cups drained pitted ripe olives

3 quarts lightly packed, rinsed crisp baby spinach leaves

½ cup shelled cooked crab, or imitation crabmeat, warmed

Salt to taste

4 SERVINGS

Warm Scallop Salad

INGREDIENTS

2½ cups uncooked gemelli pasta

6 cups shredded napa cabbage

4 whole green onions, thinly sliced

¼ cup rice vinegar, or white
   wine vinegar

3 tablespoons salad oil, divided

2 tablespoons soy sauce

1 tablespoon honey

½ teaspoon crushed red pepper

12 ounces sea scallops

4 whole romaine lettuce leaves,
   for garnish

2 tablespoons sesame seed, toasted

4 SERVINGS

Cook pasta according to package directions; drain. Rinse with cold water and drain again. Toss pasta, cabbage and onions in a large bowl. Divide salad among 4 individual salad plates.

Mix vinegar, 2 tablespoons salad oil, soy sauce, honey and red pepper in a small container; set aside.

Heat remaining oil in a nonstick skillet over medium heat. Add scallops; cook and stir about 2 minutes or until opaque.

To serve, place romaine leaves on top of each pasta salad. Place scallops in romaine leaves. Drizzle with dressing over all and sprinkle with toasted sesame seed. Serve. Refrigerate leftovers.

Other types of pasta may be used for this seafood salad.

One serving contains approximately: Calories 296, Fat 21g, Carbohydrates 30g, Protein 28g

Warm Shrimp Pasta Salad

Cook pasta according to package directions; drain and keep warm.

Heat oil and 2 tablespoons salad dressing in a large nonstick skillet over medium heat. Add shrimp; cook and stir until shrimp are pink in color and cooked through, about 3 minutes. Remove from skillet; keep warm. Discard any residue from skillet.

Add broth, 2 tablespoons salad dressing, garlic powder, black pepper and salt to same skillet; heat thoroughly over medium heat. Add Neufchatel cheese; cook and stir until melted, about 2 minutes. Stir in grape tomatoes; cook 1 minute. Stir in warm, drained pasta, Parmesan cheese and 1 tablespoon chopped basil.

Line 4 shallow bowls with salad greens. Place equal amounts pasta mixture over greens. Top each equally with warm shrimp; sprinkle with remaining chopped basil. Serve immediately. Refrigerate leftovers.

Serve this creamy shrimp meal, rich in tomato, with warm French bread.

Variation: Use chopped fresh parsley instead of chopped basil.

One serving contains approximately: Calories 550, Fat 17g, Carbohydrates 54g, Protein 42g

INGREDIENTS

3 cups uncooked bow tie pasta

1 teaspoon cooking oil

¼ cup sun-dried tomato vinaigrette salad dressing, divided

1 pound fresh peeled and deveined medium-size shrimp, tails removed

1 cup fat-free reduced-sodium chicken broth

½ teaspoon garlic powder

½ teaspoon ground black pepper

¼ teaspoon salt, or to taste

4 ounces Philadelphia Neufchatel cheese, cubed

2 cups grape tomatoes

½ cup shredded Parmesan cheese

2 tablespoons chopped fresh basil leaves, divided

Mixed baby salad greens

4 SERVINGS

Warm Sole Salad

INGREDIENTS

3 boneless skinless sole fillets (6-ounces total), cut crosswise into 8 pieces

½ teaspoon sea salt, divided

¼ teaspoon ground black pepper, divided

1 tablespoon all-purpose flour

2 tablespoons extra virgin olive oil, divided

1½ tablespoons Dijon mustard

1½ tablespoons fresh lemon juice

¼ teaspoon granulated sugar

1 large head bibb lettuce, torn into bite-size pieces

2 cups total, thinly sliced carrots, fennel and/or snow peas

4 SERVINGS

Season fish with ¼ teaspoon salt and ⅛ teaspoon pepper, then dust all over with flour. Heat 1 tablespoon olive oil in a large nonstick skillet over medium-high heat. Add fish to hot skillet in a single layer. Cook until golden brown, turning once, about 2 to 3 minutes. Place on a plate; keep warm.

Whisk mustard, lemon juice, 1 tablespoon olive oil, sugar, ¼ teaspoon salt and ⅛ teaspoon pepper in a large bowl until blended. Add lettuce and thinly sliced vegetables; toss to coat. Place equal amounts of salad on individual salad plates. Top each equally with warm fish. Serve immediately.

Serve this low-cal salad along with crusty rolls.

One serving contains approximately: Calories 150, Fat 8g, Carbohydrates 10g, Protein 11g

Zoe's Crab and Pasta Salad

Cook pasta following package directions, omitting the salt; drain and place in a large serving bowl.

Heat 1 tablespoon oil in a heavy 10-inch skillet. Add red bell pepper and garlic; stir and cook just until limp, about 2 minutes. Add green onions. Stir and cook 30 seconds; add mixture to bowl. Add crabmeat and lettuce to bowl; mix until combined.

Whisk 1 tablespoon oil, soy sauce, vinegar, wine, sugar and cayenne in a small container. Pour mixture over pasta mixture; toss gently. Serve immediately. Refrigerate leftovers.

Save this pretty salad for a special dinner. Serve with crusty garlic bread.

Variation: Use thawed frozen crabmeat or canned, instead of fresh.

One serving contains approximately: Calories 290, Fat 9g, Carbohydrates 37g, Protein 14g

INGREDIENTS

6 ounces uncooked vermicelli, or other thin pasta

2 tablespoons cooking oil, divided

1 red bell pepper, seeded and cut into matchstick strips

2 large cloves garlic, finely chopped

3 green onions, thinly sliced

6 ounces fresh lump crabmeat, picked over and bits of shell and cartilage removed

1 small head romaine or other lettuce, torn into bite-size pieces

2 tablespoons low-sodium soy sauce

2 tablespoons red wine vinegar

1 tablespoon dry sherry or white wine

½ teaspoon granulated sugar

⅛ teaspoon cayenne pepper

4 SERVINGS

beef

Beef Fajita Salad

Mix mayonnaise and salsa in a small container; set aside.

Lightly brush beef and vegetables with olive oil. Grill or broil until beef is to desired doneness and vegetables are tender.

Cut beef and red bell peppers into strips. Place warm tortillas on four individual plates. Top each tortilla with lettuce and arrange beef and vegetables over the top. Serve as desired with creamy salsa dressing. Refrigerate leftovers.

Beef strips grilled or broiled makes a good supper.

One serving contains approximately: Calories 290, Fat 3g, Carbohydrates 20g, Protein 23g

Dressing

½ cup mayonnaise

½ cup prepared salsa

½ pound beef flank steak

2 medium-size red bell peppers, quartered

1 small fresh zucchini, cut lengthwise into 4 pieces

1 red onion, cut into wedges and placed on skewers

2 tablespoons olive oil

Lettuce leaves

4 fajita-size flour tortillas, warmed

4 SERVINGS

Chili Bean Taco Salad

INGREDIENTS

2 tablespoons cooking oil

1 teaspoon chili powder

½ teaspoon salt

4 6-inch corn tortillas, cut into strips
2 inches long by ½ inch wide

1 10-ounce package mixed
salad greens

1 cup shredded Cheddar cheese

2 firm ripe tomatoes, cut into wedges

1 ripe avocado, peeled, pitted
and cubed

1 pound lean ground beef seasoned
with ¼ teaspoon salt and
¼ teaspoon ground black pepper

1 15-ounce can spicy chili beans,
undrained

½ cup sour cream

4 SERVINGS

Heat oil in a large nonstick skillet over medium-high heat. Add chili powder, salt and tortilla pieces. Cook, stirring constantly, until crisp, about 3 minutes; drain on paper towels. Place in a large bowl; cool.

Add salad greens, cheese, tomatoes and avocado to bowl with cooled tortilla pieces. Toss lightly.

Stir and cook beef in the same skillet, over medium-high heat, until meat is no longer pink, about 8 minutes; drain. Stir in beans and continue cooking until thoroughly warm.

Line 4 salad bowls with equal amounts of salad green mixture. Top each equally with beef mixture. Garnish equally with sour cream. Serve. Refrigerate leftovers.

Serve with chunky salsa and extra sour cream!

One serving contains approximately: Calories 673, Fat 41g, Carbohydrates 42g, Protein 37g

Chili Mac Salad

Season beef lightly with salt and black pepper. Cook and stir in a large nonstick skillet over medium-high heat until browned and fully cooked; drain fat. Add onion, bell pepper and garlic and continue stirring and cooking 2 minutes. Stir in remaining ingredients except cheese and salad greens. Season with salt and black pepper to taste. Cover and simmer 10 minutes.

Spoon mixture into salad bowls over mixed salad greens. Top with cheese and serve immediately. Refrigerate leftovers.

Serve with crisp crackers or hard rolls.

One serving contains approximately: Calories 225, Fat 9g, Carbohydrates 25g, Protein 14g

INGREDIENTS

12 ounces lean ground beef

½ cup chopped yellow onion

½ cup chopped green bell pepper

4 cloves fresh garlic, chopped

2 cups cooked elbow macaroni

1 16-ounce can kidney beans, rinsed and drained

1 8-ounce can whole kernel corn, drained

1 8-ounce can tomato sauce

1 14-ounce can chopped tomatoes, undrained

1 tablespoon chili powder

1 teaspoon ground cumin

½ teaspoon dried oregano

Salt and black pepper to taste

8 cups mixed salad greens

¾ cup shredded Cheddar cheese

10 SERVINGS

Confetti Taco Salad

INGREDIENTS

1 pound fresh ground beef

1 package taco seasoning mix

3 cups coarsely crushed tortilla chips

1 cup shredded Cheddar cheese

1 ripe large tomato, chopped

1 12-ounce package mixed salad greens (about 8 cups)

Sliced ripe olives

Sliced red onion

Ranch or French salad dressing, optional

4 SERVINGS

Cook and stir beef in a large nonstick skillet over medium heat for about 10 minutes, or until an internal temperature of 160°F is reached; drain and discard fat. Stir in amount of taco seasoning according to package directions for 1 pound beef. Place beef mixture in a large bowl. Add chips, cheese and tomato; toss.

Line 4 plates with equal amounts of salad greens. Top equally with beef mixture, olives, onion and salad dressing. Serve. Refrigerate leftovers

Beef taco salads are a favorite meal at our house.

One serving contains approximately: Calories 554, Fat 32g, Carbohydrates 3g, Protein 34g

Creamy Beef Taco Salad

Cook and stir meat in a large nonstick skillet over medium heat until cooked through and no longer pink; drain fat. Stir in half of taco seasoning. Spoon mixture into a large bowl.

Add shredded lettuce, tomatoes, onion and cheese. Mix salad dressing, lemon juice and remaining taco seasoning in a small container; pour mixture over salad. Toss to coat. Line 4 salad bowls with butter lettuce and top equally with salad mixture. Serve immediately. Refrigerate leftovers.

Serve topped with crushed tortilla chips or corn chips as desired.

One serving contains approximately: Calories 677, Fat 46g, Carbohydrates 5g, Protein 35g

INGREDIENTS

1 pound ground beef, seasoned with ¼ teaspoon salt and ¼ teaspoon ground black pepper

1 1.25-ounce package taco seasoning, divided

1 head iceberg lettuce, shredded

4 ripe tomatoes, seeded and diced

¾ cup chopped yellow onion

2 cups shredded Cheddar cheese

1 cup salad dressing

1 teaspoon fresh lemon juice

Butter lettuce

4 SERVINGS

Deli Beef Salad with Horseradish Dressing

INGREDIENTS

1½ pounds fresh broccoli, cut into florets; stems peeled and cut into ¼-thick slices

¾ pound thick-sliced deli roast beef, cut into ½-inch pieces

3 cups halved cherry tomatoes

6 green onions, thinly sliced

Dressing

2 tablespoons white wine vinegar

2 teaspoons Dijon mustard

½ teaspoon purchased prepared horseradish

¾ teaspoon salt

⅛ teaspoon ground black pepper

½ cup extra virgin olive oil

3 tablespoon sour cream

4 SERVINGS

Cook broccoli in a steamer basket over boiling water until tender, about 4 minutes. Drain and cool completely. Place into a large bowl. Add roast beef, cherry tomatoes and green onions to bowl.

Dressing: Whisk vinegar, mustard, horseradish, salt and pepper in a bowl. Continue whisking, slowly adding olive oil until smooth. Whisk in sour cream.

Add dressing to bowl with beef mixture. Toss to coat. Place equal amounts on 4 dinner plates and serve immediately. Refrigerate leftovers.

Variation: Leftover roast beef. Serve with rye rolls.

One serving contains approximately: Calories 436, Fat 33g, Carbohydrates 17g, Protein 24g

Grilled Pepper Steak Salad

Rub 2 teaspoons garlic and the black pepper over steak. Grill over medium heat on a covered grill, 3 to 5 minutes per side for medium doneness, depending on thickness of steak. Let steak rest a few minutes on a cutting board, then cut steak crosswise into thin slices.

Mix lettuce, tomato, avocado, 1 cup cheese and red onion in a large bowl.

Mix olive oil, lemon juice, remaining garlic and chipotle chiles in a small container until blended; add mixture to lettuce mixture and toss to coat.

Divide salad among 4 salad bowls. Top each equally with steak. Sprinkle each with remaining cheese. Serve immediately. Refrigerate leftovers.

Use mixed salad greens instead of romaine lettuce, if desired.

One serving contains approximately: Calories 488, Fat 34g, Carbohydrates 11g, Protein 35g

INGREDIENTS

2½ teaspoons minced garlic, divided

1 teaspoon ground black pepper

1 pound lean skirt steak

8 cups packed torn romaine lettuce

1 large tomato, seeded and chopped

1 ripe avocado, peeled, pitted and diced

1¼ cups shredded Cheddar cheese, divided

¼ cup thinly sliced red onion

2 tablespoons extra virgin olive oil

1 tablespoon fresh lemon juice or white wine vinegar

2 teaspoons pureed chipotle chiles in adobo sauce, optional

4 SERVINGS

Hamburger Salad

INGREDIENTS

⅓ **pound lean ground beef**

1 **small yellow onion, finely chopped**

¾ **cup canned kidney beans, rinsed**

½ **cup low-sodium V8 juice**

1 **tablespoon chili powder**

¼ **teaspoon granulated sugar**

⅛ **teaspoon salt**

⅛ **teaspoon ground black pepper**

2 **cups shredded iceberg lettuce**

½ **cup shredded low-fat Cheddar cheese**

2 **tablespoons sliced ripe olives**

2 SERVINGS

Cook and stir meat and onion in a nonstick skillet over medium heat until meat is no longer pink; drain well. Add beans, V8 juice, chili powder, sugar, salt and black pepper; cook and stir until heated through.

Line 2 salad bowls equally with lettuce. Top each with warm beef mixture, cheese and olives. Serve immediately. Refrigerate leftovers.

This is a quick supper for two . . . yes, you can double it.

One serving contains approximately: Calories 339, Fat 13g, Carbohydrates 27g, Protein 30g

Moose's Easy Taco Salad

Cook ground beef and onions with seasoning mix and water in a large skillet according to seasoning mix package directions.

Stir in corn and cheese; cover and cook on low heat about 5 minutes or until cheese is completely melted. Remove from heat; stir to blend well.

Line 6 salad bowls equally with lettuce. Spoon beef mixture equally over lettuce. Top each equally with tomatoes. Top with tortilla chips as desired. Serve immediately. Refrigerate leftovers.

Serve with a side of warm refried beans.

One serving contains approximately: Calories 460, Fat 25g, Carbohydrates 38g, Protein 24g

INGREDIENTS

1 pound lean ground beef

½ cup chopped yellow onion

1 1.25-ounce package taco seasoning mix

¾ cup water

1 10-ounce package frozen corn

8 ounces Velveeta cheese, cut into ½-inch cubes

6 cups shredded iceberg lettuce

2 ripe tomatoes, chopped

9 cups tortilla chips

6 SERVINGS

Nebraska Steak Salad

INGREDIENTS

Dressing

¼ cup extra virgin olive oil

1 tablespoon fresh lemon juice

2 teaspoons lemon pepper seasoning

2 teaspoons Dijon mustard

2 cloves fresh garlic, crushed

1 (about 1¼ pounds) boneless beef top sirloin steak (fat trimmed), cut in half lengthwise, then cut crosswise into ½-inch-thick strips

1 10-ounce package torn mixed salad greens

¼ cup grated Parmesan cheese

4 SERVINGS

Mix all dressing ingredients in a small container; reserve 2 tablespoons for salad greens. Pour remaining dressing in a medium bowl. Add steak strips; toss to coat.

Heat a large nonstick skillet over medium-high heat until hot. Add beef strips, one-half at a time. Cook and stir 2 to 3 minutes or until outside surface is no longer pink (do not over cook). Remove from skillet with a slotted spoon; keep warm.

Mix salad greens in a large bowl with reserved salad dressing and Parmesan cheese and toss to coat; line 4 individual plates with greens. Arrange beef over each. Serve immediately. Refrigerate leftovers.

Nothing satisfies like a good steak meal. Serve with crusty bread.

One serving contains approximately: Calories 350, Fat 21g, Carbohydrates 3g, Protein 36g

Quarter-Pound Beef Salad

Season beef with salt and pepper. Cook and stir in a large nonstick skillet over medium-high heat until beef is browned and fully cooked; drain fat. Add barbecue sauce, tomatoes and pickles to meat in skillet; cook and stir until heated through, about 2 minutes.

Line 4 salad plates equally with lettuce. Top each equally with meat mixture, then top each with 1 slice of onion and 1 slice of cheese. Serve immediately. Refrigerate leftovers.

Cheeseburger! Serve with fries or potato chips.

One serving contains approximately: Calories 280, Fat 11g, Carbohydrates 17g, Protein 28g

INGREDIENTS

1 pound extra-lean ground beef

½ teaspoon salt

¼ teaspoon ground black pepper

½ cup barbecue sauce

2 firm ripe tomatoes, chopped

⅓ cup chopped dill pickles

8 cups shredded iceberg lettuce

4 thin slices yellow onion

4 slices American cheese

4 SERVINGS

Roast Beef Salad

INGREDIENTS

½ pound cooked roast beef, cut into thin strips

2 cups halved cherry tomatoes

1 ripe avocado, peeled, pitted and diced

¼ cup thinly sliced red onion

3 hard-boiled eggs, sliced

1 10-ounce bag mixed salad greens

½ cup Thousand Island salad dressing

4 SERVINGS

Place all ingredients except salad dressing in a large bowl. Gently mix to combine; place equal amounts on 4 plates. Drizzle each with salad dressing. Serve. Refrigerate leftovers.

Serve with warm onion rolls.

One serving contains approximately: Calories 360, Fat 24g, Carbohydrates 14g, Protein 24g

Steak and Goat Cheese Salad

Heat a large skillet or grill pan over medium-high heat. Brush steak all over with ½ tablespoon vinaigrette; add to skillet and cook, turning once, to desired doneness, about 4 to 5 minutes total. Remove from heat. Let rest a few minutes, then slice thinly across the grain.

Toss lettuce, carrot and remaining vinaigrette in a large bowl; place on a dinner plate. Top salad with cooked steak; sprinkle with cheese. Serve immediately. Refrigerate leftovers.

This meal is just for you . . . served along with warm bread, of course!

One serving contains approximately: Calories 330, Fat 20g, Carbohydrates 13g, Protein 24g

INGREDIENTS

1 3-ounce beef sirloin flap steak, or other beef steak

2½ tablespoons purchased balsamic vinaigrette, divided

3 cups chopped romaine lettuce

1 fresh carrot, peeled and shaved into thin strips

1 ounce crumbled goat cheese

1 SERVING

Tangy Steak Salad

INGREDIENTS

1½ pounds ¾-inch-thick beef top sir-loin steak, lightly seasoned with salt and ground black pepper

6 tablespoons extra virgin olive oil, divided

1 pound button mushrooms, cleaned and sliced

1 tablespoon Dijon mustard

¼ cup white vinegar

¼ teaspoon salt

¼ teaspoon garlic powder

¼ teaspoon ground black pepper

8 cups torn romaine lettuce

6 SERVINGS

Grill steak, covered, over medium-high heat for 4 minutes. Turn steak over; brush with 1 tablespoon olive oil. Grill 4 minutes more or to desired doneness. Slice cooked steak thinly across the grain. Place in a large bowl; cover with foil and keep warm.

Put 1 tablespoon oil in a large nonstick skillet. Add mushrooms; cook and stir until tender, about 3 minutes. Remove skillet from heat. Stir in remaining oil, mustard, vinegar, salt, garlic powder and pepper. Add to bowl with steak. Stir lightly to combine.

Line 6 plates with lettuce. Top equally with steak-mushroom mixture. Serve immediately. Refrigerate leftovers.

Garnish with fresh tomato wedges. Serve with warm rolls.

One serving contains approximately: Calories 300, Fat 20g, Carbohydrates 6g, Protein 25g

Texas Beef and Bean Salad

Season beef with chili powder, cumin, salt and pepper; cook and stir in a large nonstick skillet over medium-high heat until thoroughly cooked and browned; drain and discard fat. Remove from heat.

Place remaining ingredients, except salsa, in a large bowl. Add cooked beef; mix well. Stir in salsa, if desired. Serve. Refrigerate leftovers.

Serve this tasty salad with sour cream as desired.

One serving contains approximately: Calories 674, Fat 38g, Carbohydrates 58g, Protein 29g

INGREDIENTS

1 pound lean ground beef

2 tablespoons chili powder

½ teaspoon ground cumin

¼ teaspoon salt, or to taste

¼ teaspoon ground black pepper

1 head iceberg lettuce, shredded

1 15-ounce can pinto beans, undrained

2 large ripe tomatoes, cubed

1 cup shredded Cheddar cheese

¼ cup chopped fresh cilantro or parsley

1 12-ounce package corn tortilla chips, broken

½ cup chopped green onion

1 small jalapeño pepper, seeded and chopped, optional

1 cup purchased salsa, optional

6 SERVINGS

Thai Deli Beef Salad

INGREDIENTS

Dressing

1 teaspoon fresh lime zest

3 tablespoons fresh lime juice

3 tablespoons lower-sodium fish sauce

1 tablespoon granulated sugar

1 10-ounce bag romaine salad mix

1 seedless cucumber, thinly sliced

8 ounces deli-sliced roast beef, cut into ½-inch strips

1 cup fresh cilantro

Half of a medium-size red onion, thinly sliced

4 SERVINGS

Stir lime zest, lime juice, fish sauce and sugar in a small bowl until sugar is completely dissolved.

Toss salad mix, cucumber, roast beef, cilantro and onion in large bowl. Add dressing to bowl; toss. Serve. Refrigerate leftovers.

Meat from the deli makes this tasty meal. Serve with hard rolls.

One serving contains approximately: Calories 105, Fat 2g, Carbohydrates 9g, Protein 13g

Warm Beef Bow Tie Salad

Cook pasta according to package directions; drain. Place in a large bowl.

Cook and stir beef in a medium-size nonstick skillet until browned and fully cooked; drain fat and discard. Stir in beans, chili powder and cumin; heat until thoroughly warm. Add to pasta in bowl. Add tomatoes, corn, bell pepper, cheese and onions.

Mix yogurt and salsa in a small container; add to pasta mixture; mix well. Serve. Refrigerate leftovers.

Serve this tasty family meal warm or cold.

One serving contains approximately: Calories 425, Fat 12g, Carbohydrates 57g, Protein 22g

INGREDIENTS

8 ounces uncooked bow tie pasta

8 ounces lean ground beef, seasoned with ¼ teaspoon salt

1 16-ounce can pinto beans

1 teaspoon chili powder

⅛ teaspoon ground cumin

2 fresh tomatoes, seeded and chopped

2 8-ounce cans whole kernel corn, drained

1 small green bell pepper, chopped

½ cup shredded Cheddar cheese

½ cup sliced green onions

1 cup low-fat plain yogurt

½ cup medium salsa

6 SERVINGS

Warm Steak Salad

INGREDIENTS

¾ **pound flank steak seasoned with ½ teaspoon salt and ¼ teaspoon ground black pepper**

2 cups chopped red cabbage

1 head romaine lettuce, coarsely chopped

1 15-ounce can white beans, drained and rinsed

½ cup chopped roasted peppers or fresh red bell pepper

¼ cup chopped fresh flat-leaf parsley

1 tablespoon chopped yellow onion

¼ cup Italian salad dressing

4 SERVINGS

Broil steak on a baking sheet for about 5 minutes on each side for medium-rare. Remove from broiler and cut meat into bite-size pieces.

Mix remaining ingredients except salad dressing in a large bowl. Add warm steak and salad dressing; toss to combine. Serve immediately. Refrigerate leftovers.

Other cuts of steak can be used, if desired.

One serving contains approximately: Calories 252, Fat 92g, Carbohydrates 18g, Protein 23g

Zesty Beef Salad

Cook and stir ground beef in a nonstick skillet over medium heat until no longer pink and well browned; drain well and place in a large bowl.

Add remaining ingredients except salad dressing to bowl; mix well.

Add salad dressing; toss to coat well. Serve immediately. Refrigerate leftovers.

Italian dressing adds zip to this quick salad.

One serving contains approximately: Calories 610, Fat 47g, Carbohydrates 14g, Protein 33g

INGREDIENTS

1 pound ground beef seasoned with ¼ teaspoon ground black pepper

3 cups crushed tortilla chips

2 cups shredded mozzarella cheese

2 cups shredded Cheddar cheese

1 10-ounce package mixed salad greens

1 8-ounce bottle Italian salad dressing, or to taste

6 SERVINGS

pork

Bean and Bacon Salad

Put bacon, beans, cabbage, celery, onion and parsley in a large bowl.

Mix vinegar, mayonnaise, sugar, salt and pepper in a small container until blended. Add to bacon mixture; toss until coated. Cover and chill slightly before serving. Refrigerate leftovers.

Crunchy cabbage is used in this tasty salad.

One serving contains approximately: Calories 301, Fat 21g, Carbohydrates 18g, Protein 10g

INGREDIENTS

10 slices bacon, crisply cooked, drained and crumbled

1 15-ounce can kidney beans, rinsed and drained

1½ cups shredded cabbage

½ cup diced celery

⅓ cup chopped onion

2 tablespoons chopped fresh parsley

2 tablespoons white vinegar

½ cup mayonnaise

2 tablespoons granulated sugar

1 teaspoon salt

¼ teaspoon ground black pepper

6 SERVINGS

BLT Pasta Salad

INGREDIENTS

8 ounces uncooked rotini pasta

1 pound bacon, cooked crisp, drained and cut into bite-size pieces

3 ripe tomatoes, chopped

2 cups shredded mild Cheddar cheese

¾ cup Italian salad dressing

½ cup light mayonnaise

Half of a head of iceberg lettuce, cut into 1-inch chunks

8 SERVINGS

Cook pasta according to package directions; drain and rinse with cold water, then drain again. Place in a large bowl. Add bacon, tomatoes and cheese; mix well.

Mix salad dressing and mayonnaise in a small container; add to pasta mixture and stir to coat. Cover and chill slightly. Stir in lettuce just before serving. Refrigerate leftovers.

Bacon lovers, this one's for you!

One serving contains approximately: Calories 547, Fat 46g, Carbohydrates 14g, Protein 29g

Dilled Ham Pasta Salad

Mix pasta, ham, tomatoes, onions and celery in a large bowl.

Mix salad dressing, dill and black pepper in a small container; add to bowl and toss to coat. Add cheese to bowl; toss lightly. Serve immediately or cover and chill to serve later. Refrigerate leftovers.

Serve over lettuce along with warm rolls.

One serving contains approximately: Calories 325, Fat 20g, Carbohydrates 24g, Protein 14g

INGREDIENTS

1½ cups cooked elbow macaroni or small shell pasta

1¼ cups diced fully cooked ham

1 cup halved cherry tomatoes

½ cup sliced green onions

½ cup finely chopped celery

½ cup ranch or creamy Italian salad dressing

1 tablespoon chopped fresh dill or ½ teaspoon dried dill

½ teaspoon ground black pepper

6 slices deli-style sharp Cheddar cheese, cut into ½-inch strips

6 SERVINGS

Fruited Ham Pasta Salad

INGREDIENTS

1¾ cup uncooked bow tie pasta

2 cups seedless green grapes, halved

2 cups fully cooked diced ham

½ cup chopped green onions

1½ cups diced sharp Cheddar cheese

Dressing

½ cup mayonnaise

½ cup sour cream

2 tablespoons cider vinegar

1½ tablespoons Dijon mustard

½ teaspoon granulated sugar

¼ teaspoons salt

¼ teaspoon ground black pepper

¼ teaspoon dried dill weed

8 SERVINGS

Cook pasta according to package directions; drain in a colander and rinse with cold water until cold, then drain again. Place in a large bowl. Add grapes, ham, onions and cheese to bowl.

Mix all dressing ingredients in a small bowl; add to pasta mixture and mix well. Cover and chill slightly. Serve. Refrigerate leftovers.

Serve with warm rolls.

One serving contains approximately: Calories 352, Fat 26g, Carbohydrates 18g, Protein 13g

Ground Pork Salad

Heat oil in a large nonstick skillet over medium-high heat until hot. Add pork; cook and stir until no longer pink, about 3 minutes. Add water, 1 tablespoon fish sauce and 1 teaspoon sugar; cook and stir 4 minutes or until liquid is almost gone.

Dressing: Mix lime juice, sliced jalapeño pepper, 4 tablespoons fish sauce and 2 teaspoons sugar in a small container until blended; set aside.

Line 4 salad bowls equally with lettuce. Top each with equal amounts of pork mixture, shallot, carrot, celery, mint and roasted peanuts. Drizzle with dressing as desired. Serve. Refrigerate leftovers.

Fish sauce can be found in the Asian food section.

One serving contains approximately: Calories 435, Fat 31g, Carbohydrates 16g, Protein 25g

INGREDIENTS

2 teaspoons cooking oil

1 pound ground pork

¼ cup cold water

5 tablespoons fish sauce, divided

3 teaspoons granulated sugar, divided

½ cup fresh lime juice

1 jalapeño pepper, seeded and thinly sliced

8 cups torn bibb lettuce or other lettuce

1 shallot, thinly sliced

2 carrots, coarsely grated

¼ cup thinly sliced celery

1 cup fresh mint leaves

¼ cup chopped salted roasted peanuts

4 SERVINGS

Ham and Apricot Pasta Salad

INGREDIENTS

2 cups uncooked radiatore pasta nuggets, or similar dried pasta

¾ cup low-fat mayonnaise

½ cup chopped celery

½ cup dried apricots, cut into large pieces

¼ cup sliced green onions

¼ cup diced green bell pepper

½ pound fully cooked ham, cubed

½ pound reduced-fat Swiss cheese, cubed

¼ teaspoon ground black pepper, or to taste

6 SERVINGS

Cook pasta according to package directions. Rinse with cold water until cool; drain well. Place in a large bowl.

Add remaining ingredients to bowl; mix well. Cover and chill slightly before serving. Refrigerate leftovers

Scoop this light salad over lettuce leaves. Serve with warm corn muffins.

One serving contains approximately: Calories 340, Fat 12g, Carbohydrates 36g, Protein 21g

Ham and Cheese Pasta Salad

Cook pasta according to package directions. Drain and cool; place in a large bowl. Add ham, cheese, green bell pepper, onion and olives.

Mix remaining ingredients in a small container. Pour over pasta mixture. Toss to coat. Serve. Refrigerate leftovers.

Warm Italian bread will complement this good salad.

One serving contains approximately: Calories 278, Fat 20g, Carbohydrates 15g, Protein 9g

INGREDIENTS

1 12-ounce package rotini pasta

1½ cups fully cooked ham

1 cup cubed Cheddar cheese

1 green bell pepper, seeded and diced

1 cup diced red onion

1 2¼-ounce can sliced ripe olives, drained

¾ cup creamy Italian salad dressing

½ cup ranch salad dressing

½ teaspoon ground black pepper

¼ teaspoon salt

½ teaspoon dried basil

¼ teaspoon dried oregano leaves

8 SERVINGS

Ham and Chicken Pasta Salad

INGREDIENTS

1 16-ounce package uncooked bow tie pasta

2 cups cubed fully cooked ham

2 cups cubed cooked skinless chicken breast

2 cups cubed Swiss cheese

1 cup broccoli florets

¼ cup honey

1½ cups mayonnaise

2 tablespoons Dijon mustard

2 tablespoons white vinegar

2 tablespoons finely diced yellow onion

½ cup extra virgin olive oil

¼ cup granulated sugar

¼ teaspoon salt

¼ teaspoon garlic powder

¼ grated Parmesan cheese

8 SERVINGS

Cook pasta according to package directions; drain well.

Put pasta, ham, chicken, Swiss cheese and broccoli in large bowl.

Place remaining ingredients except Parmesan cheese in a blender; process until smooth. Reserve ½ cup salad dressing mixture; pour remaining over salad in bowl. Chill slightly. Stir in remaining salad dressing and Parmesan cheese when serving. Refrigerate leftovers.

Garnish each serving with pimento stuffed olives. Serve with soft rolls.

One serving contains approximately: Calories 965, Fat 66g, Carbohydrates 61g, Protein 33g

Ham and Veggie Pasta Salad

Cook pasta and frozen vegetables in boiling water in a medium-size pot until pasta and carrots are tender, about 8 minutes. Drain in a colander, then rinse with cold water and drain well again. Place in a medium bowl. Add ham and green onions.

Mix yogurt, salad dressing and dill in a small container; pour mixture over pasta mixture. Toss until coated. Cover and chill slightly before serving.

When serving, line 4 salad plates with lettuce. Top each equally with tomato and green bell pepper. Serve. Refrigerate leftovers.

Other short tube-type pasta will work fine in this good salad.

One serving contains approximately: Calories 175, Fat 6g, Carbohydrates 16g, Protein 17g

INGREDIENTS

½ **cup uncooked orzo pasta**

1 **cup frozen mixed peas and carrots**

8 **ounces fully cooked ham, cut into ½-inch cubes**

4 **green onions, thinly sliced**

½ **cup plain low-fat yogurt**

2 **tablespoons low-fat creamy cucumber salad dressing**

¼ **teaspoon dried dill weed, or 1 teaspoon fresh chopped dill**

Lettuce leaves

2 **medium fresh tomatoes, sliced**

1 **green bell pepper, cut into half rings**

4 SERVINGS

Ham Barley Salad

INGREDIENTS

Dressing

2 tablespoons whole grain mustard

2 tablespoons finely chopped shallots

2 tablespoons red wine vinegar

6 tablespoons canola oil

¼ teaspoon brown sugar

¼ teaspoon salt

¼ teaspoon ground black pepper

3 cups water

1½ cups quick-cooking barley

3 cups thinly sliced green cabbage

4 green onions, thinly sliced

2 fresh carrots, shredded

2½ cups fully cooked ham cut into thin strips (julienned)

4 SERVINGS

Whisk all dressing ingredients in a small bowl; set aside.

Bring water to a boil in a 2-quart saucepan. Stir in barley. Reduce heat. Cover saucepan and simmer until water is absorbed, about 10 minutes. Remove from heat; let stand 2 minutes.

Mix cabbage, onions, carrots and ham in a large bowl. Add cooked, warm barley to bowl; toss. Add salad dressing; toss. Serve immediately or cover and chill to serve later. Refrigerate leftovers.

Garnish with fresh sliced tomatoes. Serve with hard rolls.

One serving contains approximately: Calories 410, Fat 18g, Carbohydrates 47g, Protein 17g

Hearty Antipasto Salad

Mix olive oil, vinegar, salt and pepper in a large bowl until blended.

Add remaining ingredients except Parmesan cheese to bowl; toss to combine. Sprinkle with Parmesan cheese. Serve. Refrigerate leftovers.

Serve with rustic Italian bread.

One serving contains approximately: Calories 370, Fat 26g, Carbohydrates 22g, Protein 14g

INGREDIENTS

¼ **cup extra virgin olive oil**

2 **tablespoons red wine vinegar**

¼ **teaspoon salt**

⅛ **teaspoon ground black pepper**

3 **cups torn romaine lettuce**

1 **15-ounce can garbanzo beans, rinsed and drained**

1 **6.5-ounce jar marinated artichoke hearts, drained and chopped**

1 **green bell pepper, chopped**

2 **ripe tomatoes, chopped**

1 **2¼-ounce can sliced ripe olives, drained**

5 **slices deli ham, chopped**

5 **thin slices hard salami, chopped**

5 **slices pepperoni, chopped**

3 **slices provolone cheese, cubed**

2 **green onions, chopped**

2 **small pickled peppers, chopped**

2 **tablespoons grated Parmesan cheese**

5 SERVINGS

Macaroni Ham Salad

INGREDIENTS

6 ounces (1½ cups) uncooked elbow macaroni pasta

1¼ cups diced fully cooked ham

1 cup halved cherry tomatoes

½ cup sliced green onions

¼ cup chopped celery

¼ cup chopped green bell pepper

½ cup ranch salad dressing

½ teaspoon dried dill weed, optional

½ teaspoon ground black pepper

6 slices sharp Cheddar cheese, cut into ½-inch strips

6 SERVINGS

Cook pasta according to package directions; drain then rinse with cold water and drain well again. Place in a large bowl. Add ham, tomatoes, onions, celery and bell pepper; toss.

Mix ranch salad dressing, dill weed and black pepper in a small container; add to pasta mixture and toss to coat. Add cheese; toss. Serve immediately. Refrigerate leftovers.

Serve over lettuce along with whole wheat rolls.

One serving contains approximately: Calories 326, Fat 20g, Carbohydrates 24g, Protein 14g

Pepperoni Ham Pasta Salad

Cook pasta according to package directions; drain; rinse with cold water then drain again. Place in a large bowl.

Add olives, tomatoes, onions, ham and pepperoni to bowl; toss. Add cheese and salad dressing; toss. Serve. Refrigerate leftovers.

This is a good choice for feeding the gang. Serve with a side of sliced cantaloupe and warm, buttered hard rolls.

One serving contains approximately: Calories 525, Fat 29g, Carbohydrates 51g, Protein 18g

INGREDIENTS

1½ **pounds uncooked seashell pasta**

1 **6-ounce can pitted black olives, chopped**

½ **cup chopped green olives**

2 **large ripe tomatoes, chopped**

3 **bunches green onions, chopped**

2 **cups chopped fully cooked ham**

4 **ounces sliced pepperoni sausage, sliced cut in half**

2 **cups shredded mozzarella cheese**

1 **16-ounce bottle Italian salad dressing, or to taste**

12 SERVINGS

Pickles and Peppers Ham Pasta Salad

INGREDIENTS

8 ounces uncooked ziti pasta

1 pound fully cooked ham, cubed

1 large green bell pepper, cut into
    1-inch pieces

1 large red bell pepper, cut into
    1-inch pieces

1 large red onion, coarsely chopped

10 small sweet pickles, chopped,
    ½-cup pickle juice reserved

1 cup fresh cherry tomatoes, halved

1 cup mayonnaise

½ cup sour cream

1 tablespoon white vinegar

½ teaspoon salt, or to taste

¼ teaspoon ground black pepper

2 fresh cloves garlic, minced

6 SERVINGS

Cook pasta according to package directions; drain. Place in a large bowl. Add ham, bell peppers, onion, chopped pickles and cherry tomatoes.

Mix mayonnaise, sour cream, vinegar, salt, black pepper, garlic and reserved juice in a small container until well blended; add to salad mixture and stir until coated. Chill slightly before serving. Refrigerate leftovers.

This hearty salad is so easy to prepare. Serve with crisp breadsticks.

One serving contains approximately: Calories 697, Fat 48g, Carbohydrates 45g, Protein 21g

Pork Taco Salad

Cook and stir pork in a large nonstick skillet over medium-high heat until no longer pink; drain. Stir in taco seasoning, beans and water. Bring to a boil. Reduce heat and simmer 5 minutes, stirring occasionally. Place mixture in a large bowl and chill in the freezer 2 minutes.

Mix lettuce, tomatoes, onion and cheese in a large bowl. Stir in chilled pork mixture. Drizzle with salad dressing; toss to coat.

Serve immediately, topped, as desired, with tortilla chips and sour cream. Refrigerate leftovers.

Use ground beef instead of pork, if preferred.

One serving contains approximately: Calories 493, Fat 30g, Carbohydrates 30g, Protein 28g

INGREDIENTS

1 pound ground pork

1 small packet taco seasoning

1 16-ounce can kidney beans, rinsed and drained

¾ cup cold water

10 cups torn romaine lettuce

2 ripe tomatoes, chopped

½ cup chopped yellow onion

2 cups shredded Cheddar cheese

½ cup Western salad dressing

Tortilla chips

Sour cream

6 SERVINGS

Pork Tenderloin Salad

INGREDIENTS

1 tablespoon cooking oil

1 pound pork tenderloin, thinly sliced

3 cloves garlic, finely chopped

Dressing

1 tablespoon brown sugar

1 tablespoon soy sauce

3 teaspoons fresh lemon juice

3 teaspoons cold water

½ teaspoon dried oregano leaves, crushed

½ teaspoon dried basil leaves, crushed

6 cups torn mixed salad greens

1 cup grape tomatoes

1 small yellow onion, thinly sliced into rings

1 red bell pepper, cut into thin strips

4 SERVINGS

Heat oil in a large nonstick skillet over medium heat. Add pork; cook and stir until no longer pink, stirring in garlic just before cooking time is up. Remove pork from skillet; keep warm.

Dressing: Stir sugar, soy sauce, lemon juice, water, oregano and basil in the same skillet. Bring to a boil; remove from heat.

Place salad greens, tomatoes, onion and bell pepper in a large bowl. Add warm, sliced pork. Pour warm dressing over all. Mix well and serve immediately. Refrigerate leftovers.

Serve this warm salad with warm onion rolls.

One serving contains approximately: Calories 458, Fat 18g, Carbohydrates 26g, Protein 50g

Prosciutto Rice Salad

Mix first eight ingredients in a large bowl.

Whisk all dressing ingredients in a small container. Pour dressing over rice mixture and mix well. Serve at room temperature or cover and chill slightly. Refrigerate leftovers.

Serve over shredded iceberg lettuce along with warm Italian bread.

One serving contains approximately: Calories 234, Fat 11g, Carbohydrates 29g, Protein 7g

INGREDIENTS

4 cups cooked white rice, cold

3 ounces diced prosciutto

1 cup red grape tomatoes

1 12-ounce jar marinated artichoke hearts, drained and cut up

3 tablespoons minced fresh flat-leaf parsley

3 tablespoons chopped fresh basil

4 green onions, finely chopped

¼ cup grated Parmesan cheese

Dressing

3 tablespoons fresh lemon juice

2 tablespoons extra virgin olive oil

2 tablespoons Dijon mustard

1 tablespoon white wine vinegar

½ teaspoon crushed dried oregano leaves

¼ teaspoon salt

¼ teaspoon ground black pepper

8 SERVINGS

Salami Pasta Salad

INGREDIENTS

3 cups uncooked penne pasta

8 ounces hard salami, cubed

½ cup chopped fresh flat-leaf parsley

4 green onions, sliced, including
   green tops

½ cup extra virgin olive oil

¼ cup cider vinegar

1 teaspoon dried oregano or
   1 tablespoon minced fresh oregano

1 teaspoon dried basil or
   1 tablespoon minced fresh basil

2 cloves garlic, minced

½ teaspoon salt, or to taste

¼ teaspoon ground black pepper

½ cup shredded Parmesan cheese

8 SERVINGS

Cook pasta according to package directions; rinse in cold water until cool and drain well. Place in a large bowl. Add salami, parsley and onions.

Mix olive oil, vinegar, oregano, basil, garlic, salt and pepper in a small container until blended. Add to pasta mixture; toss. Cover and chill slightly. Stir in cheese just before serving. Refrigerate leftovers.

Add grape tomatoes and sliced ripe olives, if desired. Garnish each serving with shredded lettuce. Serve with warm Italian rolls.

One serving contains approximately: Calories 349, Fat 24g, Carbohydrates 22g, Protein 13g

Sausage Pasta Salad

Cook pasta according to package directions; drain and rinse with cold water, then drain again. Put pasta in a large bowl. Add sausage, olives and Parmesan cheese.

Mix mayonnaise, vinegar and dressing mix in medium container. Add to pasta; stir well. Add croutons; toss. Serve. Refrigerate leftovers.

A side of fresh melon will go well with this dish.

One serving contains approximately: Calories 352, Fat 21g, Carbohydrates 32g, Protein 8g

INGREDIENTS

1 16-ounce package uncooked spiral pasta

1½ cups fully cooked thinly sliced Polish sausage

1 2.25-ounce can sliced ripe olives, drained

¼ cup shredded Parmesan cheese

1 cup mayonnaise

3 tablespoons cider vinegar

1 envelope Italian dressing mix

1 cup salad croutons

12 SERVINGS

Tangy Ham Pasta Salad

INGREDIENTS

1 cup uncooked penne pasta

1 red or green bell pepper, chopped

1½ cups pepper jack shredded cheese, divided

1 cup diced deli ham

⅓ cup thinly sliced green onions

⅓ cup sliced black or green olives

⅓ cup picante sauce

¼ cup light mayonnaise

Lettuce leaves

4 SERVINGS

Cook pasta according to package directions; drain, rinse under cold water and drain again.

Toss pasta, bell pepper, 1 cup cheese, ham, green onions and olives in a large bowl.

Mix picante sauce and mayonnaise in a small container; add to pasta mixture; toss to coat. Line 4 salad bowls with lettuce. Spoon each equally with salad mixture. Top each with remaining cheese. Serve. Refrigerate leftovers.

Serve with crusty rolls.

One serving contains approximately: Calories 340, Fat 20g, Carbohydrates 28g, Protein 14g

Warm Ham and Mushroom Bow Tie Salad

Cook pasta according to package directions; rinse and set aside.

Heat butter in a medium nonstick skillet. Add mushrooms, zucchini, bell pepper and onion; stir and cook until crisp tender, about 4 minutes.

Add cooked pasta, ham, basil, salt and black pepper; stir and cook until heated through, about 3 minutes. Remove from heat. Sprinkle top evenly with cheese; let melt. Serve immediately. Refrigerate leftovers.

Serve with a side of sliced fresh tomatoes.

One serving contains approximately: Calories 160, Fat 8g, Carbohydrates 13g, Protein 10g

INGREDIENTS

2 cups uncooked bow tie pasta

1 tablespoon butter or margarine

1 cup sliced mushrooms

1 cup sliced zucchini

1 small red bell pepper, cut into small strips

½ cup sliced onion

1 cup cubed fully cooked ham

¼ cup chopped fresh basil

½ teaspoon salt

¼ teaspoon ground black pepper

2 ¾-ounce slices Swiss cheese, cut into ¼-inch strips

4 SERVINGS

vegetarian

Asian Veggie Salad

Mix all vegetables in a large bowl. Add salad dressing; toss to coat. Serve. Refrigerate leftovers.

This quick salad is full of fresh vegetables.

One serving contains approximately: Calories 250, Fat 9g, Carbohydrates 32g, Protein 12g

INGREDIENTS

2 cups sliced napa cabbage

⅓ cup shelled edamame

⅓ cup fresh corn kernels

⅓ cup chopped red bell pepper

⅓ cup matchstick-size fresh carrot

1 baby bok choy, chopped

2 medium green onions, thinly sliced

¼ cup Asian salad dressing

2 SERVINGS

Black-Eyed Peas Salad

INGREDIENTS

2 tablespoons extra virgin olive oil

2 tablespoons red wine vinegar

3 cloves garlic, finely chopped

1 teaspoon prepared yellow mustard

Half of a fresh jalapeño pepper,
   seeded and finely chopped

1 teaspoon dried oregano

3 15-ounce cans black-eyed peas,
   rinsed and drained

1 4-ounce jar pimento peppers,
   drained

½ cup grape tomatoes

1 orange bell pepper, seeded
   and chopped

1 cup sliced green onions

Half of a red onion, diced

2 ribs celery, chopped

3 tablespoons chopped fresh
   flat-leaf parsley

Tabasco sauce to taste

Salt and black pepper to taste

Leaf lettuce

8 SERVINGS

Put all ingredients except lettuce in a large bowl; mix well. Cover and chill slightly. Serve over lettuce. Refrigerate leftovers.

Serve with warm buttered cornbread.

   Variation: Add 1 cup cooked pasta.

One serving contains approximately: Calories 180, Fat 5g, Carbohydrates 27g, Protein 8g

Cheesy Rice and Bean Salad

Mix rice, black beans and corn in a large bowl.

Mix oil and lime juice in a small container; pour over rice mixture.

Add cilantro; toss and chill slightly before serving. Stir in the cheese just before serving. Refrigerate leftovers.

Cooked rice can be found in the freezer section of food market. Serve this refreshing salad with a side of sliced fresh tomatoes.

One serving contains approximately: Calories 460, Fat 23g, Carbohydrates 50g, Protein 20g

INGREDIENTS

2 cups cooked rice

1 15-ounce can black beans, rinsed and drained

1 11-ounce can whole kernel corn with red and green peppers, drained

2 tablespoons vegetable oil

4 teaspoons fresh lime juice

2 tablespoons chopped fresh cilantro

1½ cups (6 ounces) cubed Cheddar cheese

4 SERVINGS

Chickpea Salad with Couscous

INGREDIENTS

1½ cups water

1 10-ounce box couscous

1 15.5-ounce can chickpeas, drained and rinsed

2 teaspoons grated orange zest

2 tablespoons extra virgin olive oil, divided

½ teaspoon salt, divided

½ teaspoon ground black pepper, divided

2 pounds firm ripe tomatoes, cut into wedges

Half of a small sweet onion, thinly sliced

¼ cup fresh mint, torn

¼ cup roasted almonds, roughly chopped

4 SERVINGS

Bring water to a boil in a saucepan; pour over top of couscous in a medium bowl. Cover bowl and let stand 5 minutes; fluff with a fork. Stir in chickpeas, orange zest, 1 tablespoon olive oil, ¼ teaspoon salt and ¼ teaspoon black pepper.

Mix tomatoes, onion, mint, ¼ teaspoon salt, ¼ teaspoon pepper and 1 tablespoon olive oil.

Spoon equal amounts of couscous mixture on 4 individual plates. Top each equally with tomato mixture. Sprinkle each with almonds. Serve. Refrigerate leftovers.

Serve with whole wheat rolls.

One serving contains approximately: Calories 508, Fat 17g, Carbohydrates 77g, Protein 18g

Couscous Salad

Place first six ingredients in a large bowl; toss.

Cook couscous according to package directions. Add hot cooked couscous to bowl with other ingredients; toss gently to mix. Stir in lemon juice and olive oil. Serve at room temperature. Refrigerate leftovers.

Garnish each serving with sliced avocados and blue corn chips.

One serving contains approximately: Calories 343, Fat 15g, Carbohydrates 40g, Protein 16g

INGREDIENTS

- ½ **cup fresh corn kernels**
- 1 **15-ounce can black beans, rinsed and drained**
- 1 **cup fresh red grape tomatoes**
- 1 **cup cubed (½-inch cubes) pepper jack cheese**
- 3 **green onions, thinly sliced (including green tops)**
- 3 **tablespoons chopped fresh cilantro**

- 1 **5.8-ounce package roasted garlic and olive oil couscous**
- 1 **tablespoon fresh lemon juice**
- 1 **tablespoon extra virgin olive oil**

5 SERVINGS

Curried Tortellini Salad

INGREDIENTS

1 10-ounce package cheese tortellini, cooked according to package directions, cooled

1 cup halved red grapes

½ cup chopped celery

¼ cup minced red onion

½ cup light mayonnaise

1½ to 2 teaspoons curry powder

¼ cup chopped fresh flat-leaf parsley

4 SERVINGS

Mix tortellini, grapes, celery and onion in a large glass bowl.

Stir mayonnaise and curry powder together in a small container; gently stir into salad. Chill slightly before serving. Sprinkle with parsley just before serving. Refrigerate leftovers.

Serve with a side of fresh ripe tomatoes and Italian-flavored breadsticks.

One serving contains approximately: Calories 350, Fat 16g, Carbohydrates 41g, Protein 10g

Edamame Pasta Salad

Cook pasta according to package directions, adding the edamame during the last 2 minutes of cooking time. Drain in colander.

Mix tomatoes, olives, basil, garlic, salt and red pepper flakes in a large bowl. Fold in pasta, edamame and feta. Serve on plates. Refrigerate leftovers.

My good friend, Ki Ki, from Blaine, Minnesota, shares this tasty recipe.

One serving contains approximately: Calories 235, Fat 7g, Carbohydrates 32g, Protein 13g

INGREDIENTS

4 ounces uncooked penne pasta

8 ounces fresh or frozen shelled edamame

1½ cups grape tomatoes, quartered

16 pitted kalamata olives, chopped

2 tablespoons chopped fresh basil leaves, or 2 teaspoons dried basil leaves

1 clove garlic, minced

¼ teaspoon salt

⅛ teaspoon dried red pepper flakes, optional

2 ounces crumbled reduced-fat feta cheese

4 SERVINGS

Fresh Strawberry and Orange Pasta Salad

INGREDIENTS

2 cups uncooked dried bow tie pasta

**⅓ cup creamy poppy seed
salad dressing**

¼ cup mayonnaise

¼ cup sliced green onions

**1 11-ounce can Mandarin oranges,
drained**

1 cup sliced fresh strawberries

Toasted sliced almonds, optional

4 SERVINGS

Cook pasta according to package directions; drain in a colander and cool.

Mix salad dressing and mayonnaise in a large bowl. Add cooled pasta and onion; toss to combine. Gently stir in oranges and strawberries. Sprinkle with almonds, if desired. Serve immediately. Refrigerate leftovers.

Serve with crisp cheese breadsticks.

One serving contains approximately: Calories 380, Fat 19g, Carbohydrates 46g, Protein 6g

Fried Green Tomato Salad

Place flour in a shallow dish. Whisk eggs and water in another shallow dish just until combined. Place cornmeal in another shallow dish. Sprinkle tomatoes with salt and pepper. Coat each slice with flour; shake off excess and dip into egg mixture, then coat with cornmeal.

Heat oil in a large nonstick skillet over medium-high heat. Add coated tomatoes, half at a time, and cook until done, about 4 minutes, turning once halfway through cooking. Drain on paper towels.

Line 6 salad bowls equally with salad greens. Top each equally with fried tomatoes, black-eyed peas, radishes, red onion, pecans and salad dressing.

Serve with warm corn muffins . . . buttered, of course.

One serving contains approximately: Calories 322, Fat 19g, Carbohydrates 31g, Protein 10g

INGREDIENTS

¼ cup all-purpose flour

2 eggs, slightly beaten

1 tablespoon cold water

½ cup cornmeal

3 medium green tomatoes, cut into ½-inch slices

½ teaspoon salt

¼ teaspoon ground black pepper

¼ cup cooking oil

8 cups torn mixed salad greens

1 15-ounce can black-eyed peas, rinsed and drained

⅔ cup sliced radishes

Half of a small red onion, cut into thin rings

⅓ cup chopped toasted pecans

⅔ cup ranch salad dressing

6 SERVINGS

Fruited Spinach Salad

INGREDIENTS

4 cups fresh baby spinach

1 cup canned Mandarin oranges, drained

1 cup seedless red grapes, halved

½ cup crumbled feta cheese

¼ cup toasted chopped walnuts

2 green onions, chopped

½ cup olive oil and vinegar salad dressing, or to taste

4 SERVINGS

Mix all ingredients except salad dressing in a large bowl; toss to combine.

Drizzle with salad dressing; toss to coat. Serve. Refrigerate leftovers.

Variation: Use mixed spring greens. Serve with crisp breadsticks.

One serving contains approximately: Calories 470, Fat 32g, Carbohydrates 38g, Protein 12g

Garden Pasta Salad

Cook pasta according to package directions. Drain in a colander and rinse with cold water then drain again. Place in a large bowl. Add all remaining salad ingredients to bowl; stir to combine.

Mix all dressing ingredients except Parmesan cheese in a medium bowl. Pour over salad mixture. Toss to coat. Sprinkle with Parmesan cheese. Serve. Refrigerate leftovers.

Serve over leaf lettuce along with warm multigrain rolls.

One serving contains approximately: Calories 420, Fat 26g, Carbohydrates 36g, Protein 13g

INGREDIENTS

3 cups uncooked medium-size pasta shells

2 cups broccoli florets

2 cups sliced fresh zucchini

½ cup chopped yellow onion

1 medium-size red bell pepper, cut into thin strips

1 cup cubed Cheddar cheese

Dressing

½ cup oil

3 tablespoons fresh lemon juice

2 tablespoons coarse Dijon mustard

1 teaspoon Worcestershire sauce

½ teaspoon salt

¼ teaspoon ground black pepper

1 large clove garlic, finely chopped

2 tablespoons grated Parmesan cheese

6 SERVINGS

Greek Pasta Salad

INGREDIENTS

10 ounces uncooked medium
   shell pasta

2½ cups diced ripe tomatoes

1 cup green bell pepper, cut into
   matchstick strips

Half of a medium-size red onion,
   thinly sliced

4 ounces feta cheese, crumbled

⅓ cup Greek black olives, pitted

⅓ cup low-fat vinaigrette, or to taste

¼ cup chopped fresh dill

2 tablespoons fresh lemon juice

6 SERVINGS

Cook pasta according to package directions. Drain and rinse with cold water then drain again. Place in a large bowl.

Add remaining ingredients to bowl; toss until combined. Serve at room temperature. Refrigerate leftovers.

Other types of short pasta will work fine for this tasty salad.

One serving contains approximately: Calories 154, Fat 6g, Carbohydrates 19g, Protein 6g

Greek Tabbouleh Salad

Bring water to a boil over high heat in a 2-quart saucepan. Stir in bulgur. Reduce heat to low. Cover saucepan and simmer until tender, about 5 minutes. Pour bulgur into a fine wire mesh strainer and rinse with cold water until cool; drain well.

Drain artichokes in a small container. Add 2 tablespoons cold water, vinegar, mint and olive oil; mix well. Add one-third of dressing mixture to a large bowl. Stir in artichoke hearts, garbanzos, cucumber and salad greens until coated; place equal amounts on 3 dinner plates.

Mix drained bulgur and remaining salad dressing mixture in another bowl. Place equal amounts over greens. Sprinkle equally with cheese. Season with salt and pepper to taste.

Artichokes, beans and spring greens are in this tasty salad.

One serving contains approximately: Calories 325, Fat 19g, Carbohydrates 34g, Protein 11g

INGREDIENTS

1½ **cups water**

⅔ **cup bulgur**

1 **6-ounce jar marinated artichoke hearts**

2 **tablespoons cold water**

¼ **cup white wine vinegar**

¼ **cup chopped fresh mint**

2 **tablespoons extra virgin olive oil**

1 **15-ounce can garbanzo beans, rinsed, drained**

1 **small cucumber, thinly sliced**

1 **5-ounce package spring greens salad mix**

⅓ **cup crumbled feta cheese**

Salt and black pepper to taste

3 SERVINGS

Hazelnut Fruit and Cheese Salad

INGREDIENTS

2 tablespoons fresh lemon juice

2 teaspoons granulated sugar

¼ cup hazelnut oil, or vegetable oil

3 cups torn mixed salad greens

1¼ cups shredded mild Cheddar
cheese

½ cup shredded Parmesan cheese

1½ cups fresh orange sections

1 cup fresh grapefruit sections

1 cup seedless green grapes

1 8-ounce can water chestnuts,
drained

⅛ cup toasted chopped hazelnuts

4 SERVINGS

Mix lemon juice and sugar in a small bowl. Whisk in oil until smooth and thickened; set aside.

Mix remaining ingredients except chopped hazelnuts in a large bowl. Add salad dressing; toss to coat.

Place equal amounts of salad mixture on 4 plates. Top each equally with chopped hazelnuts. Serve. Refrigerate leftovers.

Serve with fresh blueberry muffins.

One serving contains approximately: Calories 508, Fat 36g, Carbohydrates 34g, Protein 16g

Mandarin with Cashews and Cheese Salad

Place all ingredients except salad dressing in a large bowl; toss to combine. Drizzle with dressing; toss to coat. Serve. Refrigerate leftovers.

Fruit, nuts and cheese are tossed in this salad. Serve with croissants.

One serving contains approximately: Calories 548, Fat 38g, Carbohydrates 40g, Protein 16g

INGREDIENTS

1 10-ounce package hearts of romaine salad mix

1 11-ounce can mandarin oranges, drained

1 cup lightly salted cashews

¾ cup shredded Cheddar cheese

¾ cup shredded smoked Swiss cheese

½ cup dried cranberries

¾ cup poppy seed salad dressing

5 SERVINGS

Mango Pecan Salad

INGREDIENTS

Dressing

½ teaspoon curry powder, or to taste

2 tablespoons vegetable oil

4 tablespoons rice vinegar

¼ cup non-fat plain yogurt

¾ cup mango chutney

Salad

3 ripe mangoes, peeled and diced

½ cup coarsely chopped pecans

1 cup sliced water chestnuts

4 cups mixed spring salad greens

4 SERVINGS

Mix all dressing ingredients in a small container until well blended.

Place all salad ingredients in a large bowl. Drizzle with salad dressing; toss until coated. Serve immediately. Refrigerate leftovers.

Serve this light meal with thick slices of banana bread or warm muffins.

One serving contains approximately: Calories 641, Fat 37g, Carbohydrates 80g, Protein 10g

Quinoa and Beans Salad

Bring water to a boil in a 2-quart saucepan over high heat. Stir in quinoa. Reduce heat to medium-low. Cover saucepan and simmer until tender, about 15 minutes. Spoon hot cooked quinoa into a large bowl.

Stir in remaining ingredients. Serve immediately. Refrigerate leftovers.

Garnish with sliced fresh tomatoes. Serve with whole wheat rolls.

One serving contains approximately: Calories 264, Fat 12g, Carbohydrates 31g, Protein 7g

INGREDIENTS

1 cup water

½ cup uncooked quinoa

1 15-ounce can garbanzo beans, drained

1 cup chopped fresh broccoli

2 cloves garlic, minced

1 tablespoon fresh lemon juice

1 teaspoon dried tarragon, or to taste

2 teaspoons coarse Dijon mustard

3 tablespoons extra virgin olive oil

¼ teaspoon salt

¼ teaspoon ground black pepper

4 SERVINGS

Quinoa Spinach Salad

INGREDIENTS

½ cup quinoa, rinsed

1 cup water

1 cup halved cherry tomatoes

½ cup frozen petite peas, thawed

½ cup diced fresh carrot

¼ cup diced red onion

1 tablespoon chopped fresh
   flat-leaf parsley

2 tablespoons fresh lemon juice

1 tablespoon white balsamic vinegar

2 teaspoons extra virgin olive oil

1½ teaspoons Dijon mustard

1 teaspoon dried thyme

¼ teaspoon salt

¼ teaspoon ground black pepper

2 cups fresh baby spinach

4 SERVINGS

Bring water to a boil in a 1-quart saucepan over high heat. Stir in quinoa. Reduce heat. Cover saucepan and simmer until water is absorbed, about 15 minutes. Place in a large bowl; fluff with a fork. Cool.

Add tomatoes, peas, carrot, onion and parsley to bowl.

Mix lemon juice, vinegar, olive oil, mustard, thyme, salt and pepper in a small container; add to quinoa mixture in bowl and toss to combine. Chill slightly. Serve over spinach. Refrigerate leftovers.

Garnish each serving with cubed cheese. Serve with crisp breadsticks.

One serving contains approximately: Calories 145, Fat 4g, Carbohydrates 24g, Protein 5g

Red Bean Feta Salad

Place all ingredients in a large bowl; stir gently to combine. Cover and chill slightly. Serve. Refrigerate leftovers.

Serve with whole wheat rolls.

Variation: Use garbanzo instead of kidney beans.

One serving contains approximately: Calories 245, Fat 12g, Carbohydrates 24g, Protein 12g

INGREDIENTS

1 15-ounce can red kidney beans, drained and rinsed

1 cup crumbled feta cheese

1 red bell pepper, seeded and chopped

2 cups chopped green cabbage

4 green onions, chopped

⅓ cup chopped fresh flat-leaf parsley

1 large clove garlic, minced

2 tablespoons fresh lemon juice

1 tablespoon extra virgin olive oil

Salt and black pepper to taste

4 SERVINGS

Red Quinoa Avocado Salad

INGREDIENTS

1 7-ounce package red quinoa

1 12-ounce package whole kernel corn, thawed

1 cup finely chopped fresh cilantro

1 cup green onions, thinly sliced

1 cup diced plum tomatoes

2 ripe avocados, peeled, pitted and cut into small cubes

½ cup lemon vinaigrette

½ teaspoon salt

½ teaspoon ground black pepper

10 SERVINGS

Cook quinoa according to package directions. Place in a large bowl and cool.

Gently stir in remaining ingredients until combined. Serve immediately. Refrigerate leftovers.

My good friend Yvonne from Rochester, NY, shares this tasty recipe.

One serving contains approximately: Calories 210, Fat 9g, Carbohydrates 27g, Protein 5g

Southwestern Pasta Salad

Cook pasta according to package directions. Drain. Rinse under cold water until cool, then drain well again. Place in a large bowl.

Add remaining ingredients to bowl. Mix until combined. Serve at room temperature. Refrigerate leftovers.

Black beans and zesty tomatoes flavor this good salad.

One serving contains approximately: Calories 293, Fat 8g, Carbohydrates 43g, Protein 12g

INGREDIENTS

8 ounces uncooked rotelle (wagon wheel) pasta

1 15-ounce can black beans, drained and rinsed

1 10-ounce can diced tomatoes and green chiles, undrained

1 cup reduced-fat sour cream

½ cup chopped green bell pepper

¼ cup chopped red onion

½ cup shredded reduced-fat Cheddar cheese

6 SERVINGS

Spinach and Pasta Salad

INGREDIENTS

1 9-ounce package refrigerated linguine

5 cups shredded fresh spinach leaves

1 cup chopped fresh tomatoes

1 cup halved, thinly sliced red onion

¼ cup pine nuts, or walnut pieces, toasted

1 7-ounce container refrigerated all-natural pesto with basil

½ teaspoon fresh lemon zest

3 tablespoons fresh lemon juice

¼ teaspoon salt

⅛ teaspoon ground black pepper

4 SERVINGS

Cook pasta according to package directions; rinse with cold water in a colander and drain well. Place in a large bowl.

Add spinach, tomatoes, onion and pine nuts to bowl.

Mix pesto, lemon zest, lemon juice, salt and pepper in a small container. Add to bowl; toss. Serve immediately or refrigerate. Refrigerate leftovers.

Serve with warm Italian garlic bread.

One serving contains approximately: Calories 510, Fat 30g, Carbohydrates 47g, Protein 16g

Spinach Tortellini Salad

Cook tortellini according to package directions; drain, leaving ¼ cup water with tortellini. Pour into a large bowl.

Add spinach, tomatoes, reserved oil, lemon zest and lemon juice to bowl; stir. Season with salt and pepper to taste. Place equal amounts in 4 salad bowls. Top each equally with cheese. Serve. Refrigerate leftovers.

Serve with crisp garlic-flavored breadsticks.

One serving contains approximately: Calories 485, Fat 16g, Carbohydrates 60g, Protein 23g

INGREDIENTS

2 9-ounce packages refrigerated cheese tortellini

1 5-ounce bag baby spinach

¾ cup oil-packed sun-dried tomatoes, drained and chopped, reserving 1 tablespoon drained oil

1 teaspoon fresh lemon juice

Salt and pepper to taste

2 ounces goat or feta cheese, crumbled

4 SERVINGS

Strawberry Spinach Cottage Cheese Salad

INGREDIENTS

6 ounces baby spinach

¼ cup sliced green onions

½ cup light raspberry vinaigrette

2 cups cottage cheese

1 cup sliced fresh strawberries

¼ cup chopped walnuts

4 SERVINGS

Toss spinach and onions with vinaigrette in a large bowl; place equal portions on 4 salad plates. Spoon cottage cheese equally over spinach mixture. Top each equally with strawberries and walnuts. Serve. Refrigerate leftovers.

Pick ripe strawberries for this good salad.

One serving contains approximately: Calories 242, Fat 10g, Carbohydrates 25g, Protein 17g

Summer Couscous Salad

Add water to a medium saucepan; bring to a full boil. Stir in couscous and return to a boil. Remove saucepan from heat; cover and let stand 5 minutes. Fluff couscous with a fork and spoon into a large bowl; let cool to room temperature.

Add remaining ingredients to bowl. Toss until coated. Season with salt and black pepper to taste. Serve. Refrigerate leftovers.

Stir in chopped fresh baby spinach leaves for added goodness, if desired. Garnish each serving with cherry tomatoes and fresh cucumber spears.

One serving contains approximately: Calories 310, Fat 8g, Carbohydrates 55g, Protein 9g

INGREDIENTS

1½ cups water

1 cup plain couscous

2 cups fresh corn kernels, boiled in water 3 minutes; drained

1 cup packed fresh basil leaves, finely chopped

½ cup finely diced red bell pepper

½ cup finely diced red onion

2 cloves fresh garlic, minced

2 tablespoons coarsely chopped fresh flat-leaf parsley

5 tablespoons fresh lemon juice, mixed with 2 tablespoons extra virgin olive oil

Salt and ground black pepper to taste

4 SERVINGS

Tex-Mex Chopped Salad

INGREDIENTS

1 15-ounce can black beans, drained and rinsed

2 ripe avocados, peeled, pitted and diced

2 cups halved cherry tomatoes

1 yellow bell pepper, seeded and chopped

½ cup chopped red onion

2 tablespoons chopped fresh cilantro, optional

½ cup finely shredded Mexican four-cheese blend

⅓ cup zesty Italian salad dressing

½ teaspoon ground cumin

¼ teaspoon garlic powder

6 SERVINGS

Place beans, avocados, tomatoes, bell pepper, onion cilantro and cheese in a large bowl; mix gently.

Mix salad dressing, cumin and garlic powder in a small container; add to salad mixture in bowl; stir gently to combine. Serve immediately. Refrigerate leftovers.

Top with broken tortilla chips when serving, if desired. Serve with warm cornbread or muffins.

One serving contains approximately: Calories 270, Fat 17g, Carbohydrates 24g, Protein 9g

Tofu Rice Vegetable Salad

Place rice, tofu, tomatoes, onions, bell pepper, cucumber and squash in a large bowl; toss.

Whisk vinegar and mustard in a small bowl. Whisk in olive oil, salt and pepper. Stir salad dressing mixture into rice mixture.

Cover and chill slightly. Sprinkle with chopped parsley just before serving. Refrigerate leftovers.

Add toasted chopped peanuts for extra crunch.

One serving contains approximately: Calories 492, Fat 24g, Carbohydrates 56g, Protein 18g

INGREDIENTS

3 cups cooked rice, cold

1 8-ounce package baked flavored tofu, diced

2 cups halved grape tomatoes

½ cup chopped green onions

½ cup chopped orange or green bell pepper

1 small seedless cucumber, halved lengthwise, then sliced

½ cup diced yellow squash or zucchini

2 tablespoons red wine vinegar

2 tablespoons Dijon mustard

⅓ cup extra virgin olive oil

¼ teaspoon salt

¼ teaspoon ground black pepper

2 tablespoons chopped fresh flat-leaf parsley

4 SERVINGS

Tomatoes and Cheese Pasta Salad

INGREDIENTS

1 pound uncooked bow tie pasta

1½ pounds roma tomatoes, cut into bite-size pieces

6 ounces crumbled feta cheese

½ cup pitted kalamata olives

½ cup torn fresh basil leaves

¼ cup extra virgin olive oil

2 ounces shaved Parmesan cheese

6 SERVINGS

Cook pasta according to package directions. Drain in a colander and rinse with cold water then drain again.

Mix tomatoes, feta cheese, olives, basil and olive oil in a large bowl. Add pasta; toss. Top with Parmesan cheese. Serve. Refrigerate leftovers.

Serve with warm garlic bread.

One serving contains approximately: Calories 478, Fat 25g, Carbohydrates 71g, Protein 17g

Warm Kidney Bean Salad

Heat oil in a large nonstick skillet over medium heat. Add onion; stir and cook 5 minutes. Stir in oregano, vinegar, salt and kidney beans; cook until heated through. Stir in parsley and olives. Serve. Refrigerate leftovers.

Serve with warm whole wheat rolls . . . buttered, of course.

One serving contains approximately: Calories 200, Fat 6g, Carbohydrates 29g, Protein 10g

INGREDIENTS

2 tablespoons extra virgin olive oil

2 cups slivered yellow onion

1 teaspoon dried oregano

¼ cup cider vinegar

1 teaspoon salt

2 15-ounce cans red kidney beans, rinsed and drained

1 cup chopped flat-leaf parsley

¼ cup pimento-stuffed green olives, sliced in half

6 SERVINGS

Index

About the Author

Theresa Millang is a popular and versatile cookbook author. She has written successful cookbooks on muffins, brownies, pies, cookies, cheesecake and casseroles, as well as several on Cajun cooking. She has cooked on television and contributed many recipes to food articles throughout the U.S.A.

Theresa's Other Current Cookbooks

The Best of Cajun-Creole Recipes
The Best of Chili Recipes
The Great Minnesota Hot Dish
The Joy of Apples
The Joy of Blueberries
The Joy of Cherries
The Joy of Cranberries
The Joy of Rhubarb
The Joy of Strawberries
The Joy of Peaches
The Joy of Raspberries
Cooking with Rotisserie Chicken

Theresa's Other Cookbooks

I Love Cheesecake
I Love Pies You Don't Bake
The Muffins Are Coming
The Cookies Are Coming
The Brownies Are Coming
Roux Roux Roux